To Bank Neff

Best Wishes

Saro Yfphning

4 - 3 - 96

GARO YEPREMIAN

"I Keek a Touchdown"

THE GARO YEPREMIAN STORY

GARO YEPREMIAN

"I Keek a Touchdown"

THE GARO YEPREMIAN STORY
as told to
NELSON SEARS

Published by Garnel Books

Graphics and Production coordination by
Boardroom Graphics, Lancaster, PA

Original cover art by Garo Yepremian, Jr.

Book design by Patricia R. Kahler

ISBN   0-9649963-0-8

ACKNOWLEDGEMENT

I wish to thank UNI-MARTS for making this book possible.

I'm very proud to have UNI-MARTS as a sponsor of my motivational speeches to students in schools throughout the Middle Atlantic States.

There is a hunger in the world for words and deeds that give a lasting message of hope to young Americans. The obstacles overcome, the glories and the heartaches of life in the National Football League have provided me with real life examples that prove that anyone can achieve positive goals if they have faith and perseverance.

I have known the uncertainties and oppression of hope in other countries. My faith in God and in the United States remains strong and unwavering.

For a strong sense of corporate citizenship and continuing efforts to bring a positive message to children, we dedicate this book to UNI-MARTS.

GARO YEPREMIAN

UNI-MARTS

Special Recognition to:

My parents, Azadouhi and Sarkis Yepremian
My brother Krikor. His dream aimed high.
Brother Berj for continuing support
My wife and sons, Maritza, Garo, Jr. and Azad
Maritza's parents, Vartan and Varteny Javian

To Don Shula for inspiration during and after my football career.

Shula's rules are magnified in importance as the years pass by.

To Bob Sheridan, Joey Carr and Bob Griese for long-lasting friendship.

Special thanks to Henry Sahagian and Charles "Chuck" Markam

CONTENTS

PART 2

PART 3

PROLOGUE

Don Shula's leadership, team spirit, hard work and the support of the city that loves them, empowers the Miami DOLPHINS to engrave their names in the record books of the National Football League.

The field goal seeking football travels across the threshold of unbelief. It is propelled by the rising roar of the largest crowd ever to gather in the Orange Bowl for a DOLPHINS regular game. Down the hallway of possibility the football finds its way over the lonesome valley of rejection. It cuts through the rain and swirling winds. It passes the sentinels of hope into the realm of success. The ball clears the bar squarely through the 21'6" space separating the goal posts. The roar of the crowd reverberates throughout the stadium. The rain drops merge with the suddenly released tears in his eyes. His teammates surround him for wild congratulations.

GARO YEPREMIAN, the most improbable person ever to play in the National Football League, has earned the right to be a regular member of the DOLPHINS team.

In October, 1981, the finality of his dismissal from football is a new crisis that he has to overcome to regain his self-respect. He is now a nationally recognized motivational speaker.

The harvest of the bitter years and of the sweet years is the true-to-life material for this unusual story.

NELSON SEARS

PART I ❧

Chapter 1 ❧

Garo Yepremian tosses, turns and mumbles in his fitful sleep. The demons of doubt are using his mind for a playground. Suddenly he awakens, vaguely aware of the pre-dawn sounds of the city. Searching in the darkness for his robe, he hurries to the kitchen to run away from the horrid thoughts tumbling through his brain.

"I'm worthless. There's no meaning to life.

I'm banished from everything.

Doesn't anyone care about what I gave to my teams?

Oh God! How can this be? Have you forsaken me?" He stares at the clock. It shows 4:28 A.M. The clock becomes the enemy in his battle to get through the night.

The calendar above the kitchen table tells him it is October 15th, 1981.

Three weeks, one day, four-hours and twenty-eight minutes after he is out of professional football Garo Yepremian is in the fourth stage of depression. Garo is living on the dreary side of an aching heart. He has fallen from the penthouse of popularity to the craphouse of despair.

He is not alone in his misery. Depression is shared by millions of Americans.

It strikes the executive who, at the peak of his career and self esteem, is offered a golden parachute that turns to dust in the reality of inflation.

It claims the loyal factory worker who has labored thirty-five years for his company and suddenly learns that in reverence to the God of Profitability his honest toil is no longer needed.

It fells the secretary who has spent most of her working life as a fender of protection for a series of upwardly mobile bosses. Her fragile job security is erased by big company eating little company. Heartless corporate mergers make headlines on the business pages of the daily paper.

Optimistic young people study hard to earn a college degree. They are often denied entry level work in their field of dreams. Depression lays them low in the prime of youth.

In his early morning loneliness Garo boils water to make a cup of hot mint tea to calm his churning stomach. He sips the tea and regains some control over his shaking body.

During his active football career he assumed that the streets would be paved with gold when he quit the game. His fans treasured his autograph. Businesses competed for open dates on his public speaking calendar.

He confided to family members, "After football I'll

have lots of time to take advantage of these money making and soul satisfying opportunities."

The first week after his release the sports writers and sportscasters did their customary sound bites and wrote pieces about the fallen star.

Garo said, "I'll get a call from another team that can use my talents."

Privately he reasoned that he would have an opportunity to vent his anger on his ex-coaches and team owner Joe Robbie.

In their never-ending quest for a hot story, the sports people lose interest and the calls don't come.

In the second week of his rejection the serpent of fear slithers onto the scene to override his early anger and desire to get even.

The third week of his banishment is pure hell. Too embarrassed to go out in public he is afraid to go beyond the doors of his home. In his withdrawal from reality Garo's feelings fester into self doubt. His telephone is ominously silent. His football friends' enthusiasm cools in a hurry. Garo feels forgotten and neglected by the people and the game that has been his public identity for fifteen years.

He said, "I remember the old time players who live with their broken hopes and worn out memories. I fear that I may become one of them."

Despite his loss of appetite, lack of sleep and bone weary tiredness brought on by the Freudian battle being waged in his brain, a little pearl of sanity breaks loose and floats into his conscious mind. Garo seizes that pearl and makes a decision.

"My family is the most important part of my life. I

won't accept defeat. Somehow, somewhere I'll regain
success. It won't be easy. Nothing ever is. I found that
out a long time ago."

There in Miami in the pre-dawn darkness he
thought about the ants and grasshoppers on "the wall"
in Larnaca, Cyprus. Like a camellia flower blooming
in the fallen snow a smile came on his face. He
remembers the first football game he ever saw.
Impossible as it may seem, he kicked off in that game.

The Detroit LIONS are in Baltimore to play the
fourth game on their schedule in the 1966 National
Football League season.

At 8:30 Sunday morning, a half-hour before the
team breakfast, Dr. Ronald Eshelman, the team
chaplain conducted chapel service. He talked about
how God loves everybody. He prayed for the team's
safety and thanked the Lord for his blessings on the
team. Following the chapel service Garo was stopped
at the entrance to the dining area by the woman who
was in charge. She didn't believe that Garo was
a member of the team. He was not wearing one of
the classy blue blazers with the LIONS insignia
emblazoned on the left breast pocket. There had been
no time to have him fitted for a jacket. She had to go
into the room and ask someone to vouch for him.

The team meal was an exciting experience. At
9:00 A.M., four hours before game time, the players
were eating sixteen-ounce sirloin steaks with eggs,
baked potatoes, mountains of toast and lots of butter,
orange juice, milk and coffee.

Garo says, "I was particularly impressed by the

canned Georgia peach halves being gobbled up by the players. For the first time in my life I was seeing and enjoying life in the first class lane."

From the hotel the team bus took them to Memorial Stadium.

Baltimore is a sports mad city. The ORIOLES had recently swept the Los Angeles DODGERS in four straight games to win the World Series.

The Baltimore COLTS, with the precision passing of quarterback Johnny Unitas, is a feared powerhouse in the league. The stadium is sold out and scalpers are getting premium prices. A ticket is a prized possession. The fans are eager to commit vocal mayhem in support of their team. Quarterback Johnny Unitas turns football fever up to the boiling point in Baltimore.

In the LIONS locker room the smell of liniment and wintergreen rubdown ointment fills the air. Amid the hubbub of the pregame preparation the defensive unit huddles in camaraderie and bravado in anticipation of the coming battle. They slap hands and slam their shoulder pads against each other. They are getting meaner and meaner by the minute.

Three-hundred-fifteen pound defensive tackle Roger Brown and his six-foot-three-inch two-hundred-fifty pound fellow defensive lineman Alex Karras wear their fierce game faces. It is a form of self-hypnosis that eases the pain of old injuries and the incompletely healed newer ones. The ability to play with pain is an important asset in the National Football League. Scowling and mental ferocity helps the players focus on the job ahead.

Before arriving in the locker room Garo imagined that each player would have a private place to dress for the game. Now, he looks in confusion at the strange assortment of pads, pants, shirt and helmet. He is shocked to see the other players strip naked and walk around the room to converse and get ready for the game. He has never seen so many naked people before. He thinks these black and white players look like a bunch of wild animals.

He is embarrassed. His street pants have a button fly. Under the pants he is wearing briefs rather than the boxer shorts that are in style.

Another player sees this out-of-place runt among the giant sized men. He thinks someone is pulling a lousy locker room stunt that is bound to distract his team from this important game.

He roars loud enough for the whole world to hear, "Who in the hell is that? Get that little piss ant outta here."

The words bounce off the walls. Some people stare in disbelief when they see this little man.

Members of the sports media pay careful attention to the scene.

Showing the cockiness of a bantam rooster Garo jumps up and publicly proclaims his goal, "I will become number one to match the number on my jersey."

His teammates warned, "They're gonna kill you. You'd better run out after you kick." A telegram taped to the wall of his dressing cubicle reads as follows:

* * *

GARO SARKIS YEPREMIAN   BALL PLAYER
MUNICIPAL STADIUM BALTO
CONGRATULATIONS AND GOOD LUCK
FROM   YOUR FELLOW ARMENIANS OF THE
ST. SARKIS ARMENIAN APOSTOLIC CHURCH
PASTORS AND BOARD OF TRUSTEES

Armenian pride is beginning to swell. Garo feels that he is the standard bearer.

Following his public outburst he sits there red-faced. He notices that many players are putting tape on their ankles, wrists and ribs.

He thinks, "This team is paying me a lot of money to be here. I better do what the other players are doing."

Garo says, "I took a roll of tape and wrapped my arms from the wrist to the elbow followed by a few turns around my rib cage area. I don't have much hair on my head. To make up for that, there is a luxuriant growth on my chest."

Wide receiver Bill Malinchak came over and said, "You don't need tape around your chest."

Bill and linebacker Ernie Clark ripped the tape off Garo's ribs.

Garo, "It was the most painful thing I ever experienced in the NFL."

Ernie took a close look at Garo's diminutive body and said, "I know you've only been with the team two days. Take my advice. When you kick off run to the sideline. If you don't they're gonna kill you."

Ernie took the time to show Garo how to put his inner socks on first and how to position the stirrups of his outer socks under the instep and pull them up over the inner socks. Garo didn't know anything about shoulder pads. Ernie showed him how to place them on his shoulders.

A little later Gale Cogdill, a wide receiver said, "Garo when you kick off you'd better run out."

After getting fully dressed with the LIONS emblazoned helmet on his head Garo felt nine feet tall. There had been varying reports in the newspapers about Garo's height and weight. Actually, he was five-feet-seven-inches tall and weighed one-hundred-forty-two pounds.

There was a problem with the face bar. It bothered him. He didn't think he could concentrate on the football with the bar across his face.

He said to Friday Maclem, the equipment manager, "Please take this bar off. It makes me feel closed in."

The LIONS took the field to warm up. Garo finished his routine by booting five kicks straight up the middle from the 50-yard line, against the wind.

Head Coach Harry Gilmer is in full regalia. He dresses like a cowboy and wears a big ten-gallon hat. He has a chew of tobacco in his mouth that is so big it makes his cheek puff out so that it looks deformed.

Looking at Garo he said, "Son come over here. We just loss the toss of the coin."

Garo says, "With my limited knowledge of English I didn't know what he meant. I started looking for it."

Gilmer said, "No! No! What are you looking for? Because of the loss of the coin toss you have to kick off. As soon as you kick come and stand by me."

"With all of the warnings from my teammates and

Coach Gilmer I began to think that I could get killed out there."

The teams lined up for the kickoff with Baltimore on the receiving end. The whistle blew. Garo kicked the ball with the ferocity of an underdog—a little man determined to succeed in the violent world of professional football.

Garo says, "It was a beautiful end-over-end kick deep behind the Baltimore goal posts. Blockers led the receiver up the field. Again remembering that the LIONS were paying me a lot of money, I stooped to pick up the kicking tee. When I stood up I saw a group of COLTS players headed in my direction."

He saw a helmeted stampede of human muscle and bone threatening to crash over him and ruin his dream. Garo heard the startling roar of the fans. It became an overpowering voice screaming "Kill you! Kill you!"

The words and pictures played in virtual reality on the movie screen of his mind. On the tachometer of life his heart was way above the red line.

Garo says, "The words stunned my brain and shackled my feet. My steps seemed nightmarishly slow. I headed for the sideline as fast as I could. I made it to the bench and was happy to sit down. A loud roar arose from the crowd. My teammates on the other side of the field waved for me to cross the field to their side."

In his hurry the great Garo Yepremian followed orders and ran off the field to the Baltimore side and sat on the COLTS bench.

In the rush of his tryout and the newness of it all Garo was getting a lot of advice about football. His brother, Krikor told him to listen to the public address system and when he heard "fourth down" he should be prepared to kick.

The first time he heard "fourth down" he said to Coach Gilmer, "I keek a touchdown?"

Gilmer said, "Get outta here."

Later Garo again heard the public address announcer say "fourth down."

He again approached Gilmer and said, "I keek a touchdown?"

Gilmer snorted, "Get the hell outta here. We're on our own 10-yard line."

Gilmer punctuated this outburst with a stream of tobacco juice aimed in the general direction of the Baltimore bench.

The COLTS went on to massacre the LIONS 45-14.

Johnny Unitas had one of his big days. He threw four touchdown passes and used his running game to perfection.

LIONS quarterback Milt Plum went out of the game with a torn knee ligament. He would be out for the season.

Karl Sweetan came in as backup quarterback. Karl played his college football at Wake Forrest and came to the LIONS by the way of the Pontiac ARROWS.

Standing behind the goal line Karl took a snap from center and passed to Pat Studstill who went all the way for a touchdown. It was the highlight of the day for the LIONS. Garo would have to wait for another day to attempt his first NFL field goal.

That day would bring new and fearful revelations about the game of football.

Chapter 2 ❧

To find out how this little man reached this improbable position to kick-off in the first National Football League game he ever saw we return to the year 1908.

In the sports world, the American Indian athlete Jim Thorpe is making a name for himself in football. Jim earns two-hundred-and-fifty dollars per game with the Canton BULLDOGS. That Ohio team wins ten straight games.

The league declares them champions of the world.

On the international scene, the social and economic pressures on the Armenians in Turkey are unbearable. At the beginning of the fourth century Gregory the Illuminator brought Christianity to Armenia. Consequently, Armenia was the first nation to choose the Christian faith as its national religion. As the centuries passed political and religious passions were constantly in conflict. The Armenians were eventually overrun by the Turks. They lived or died at the will and pleasure of their oppressors.

Krikor Yepremian was desperate to find work. He was willing to risk life itself to make enough money to support his family. Exciting news arrived—money could be earned in the United States.

Krikor said, "My friends we have no choice. We must go to America. We and our families will starve to death here."

Krikor and several other desperate men sailed over the awesome ocean from Turkish Armenia to New York. They continued their journey overland to Detroit, Michigan.

Krikor's wife Vartouhi remained in Turkey while he went overseas to America. A young girl at the turn of the 20th century, she was attracted to him because of his handsome good looks and adventuresome personality. Krikor's tenderness and affection changed the physical attraction into real love. His masculinity did not get in the way of his manhood. Krikor and Vartouhi said their wedding vows in Evereg, Turkey.

In Detroit, Krikor and his Armenian friends found work in the young automobile industry. The autos had many parts made of wood and Krikor was put to work tacking upholstery to the wooden door frames. It was tedious work. It took him a few days and many painful hammer hits on his fingers to learn how to drive the sharp tacks into the wood fast enough to keep up with the other workers. To fight off the monotony of the job thoughts of home and his distant family occupied his mind. With fierce determination he labored long hours in the auto assembly shop.

The winter weather was bitter cold in Detroit that year. The Armenians warmed their hands and backsides near the stove. They couldn't afford to buy firewood. Krikor chopped and burned some of the furniture and the closet doors in their rented house. In spite of the hardships Krikor saved his money and dreamed of the day when he could make a triumphant return home. After Krikor went to the United States political unrest and physical danger from the Turkish Army caused Vartouhi to move to Cyprus. In Cyprus Vartouhi endured her loneliness. She sang the songs of her people to her toddler son, Sarkis. Most of all she missed Krikor.

During her first pregnancy his love and caring helped her through the rough months. The tender moments before, during and after childbirth were treasured forever. Now that he was overseas in the far off United States her heart was aching as she yearned for the caress of her man's work hardened hands.

After what seemed to Vartouhi to be an interminable amount of time Krikor came home to Cyprus. Their reunion was pure bliss. Krikor held Sarkis in his arms and was overcome with emotion when he realized how many of the boy's growing years were lost to him forever. Following the initial ecstasy of the homecoming Vartouhi yearned to see her friends and relatives in Turkey. The time of separation and the attendant economic uncertainties were the catalyst for Vartouhi's feelings of homesickness. She begged Krikor to make the move to her ancestral home in Turkey. Krikor did not want to go. However, above all else he wanted to make Vartouhi happy. She was pregnant with her second child and his heart was full of joy. Krikor, Vartouhi, Sarkis and her parents left Cyprus and returned to Turkey. In Turkey, Vartouhi gave birth to a daughter who was named Sirarpi.

The timing of their return to Evereg, Turkey was disastrous. The guns and passions of war overran Europe and Asia Minor. Old hatreds flamed with renewed vengeance. The Turkish government organized mass deportations of the Armenians to the Syrian desert accompanied by unprecedented massacres. Genocide resulted in 1,800,000 deaths and caused another million Armenians to flee to other countries. Many of the Armenians became famous in their adopted countries. In the United States William Saroyan won the Pulitzer prize in 1939 for the play THE TIME OF YOUR LIFE. Later, Mike Conners became a well known television and movie star.

The Armenian men in Krikor's village were rounded up, ostensibly to be conscripted into the army. They were forced to climb onto trucks and the convoy headed out of the town. Krikor didn't trust the soldiers at all. He was ready to make a break at the slightest opportunity. A short distance away in the countryside the trucks halted in an open field. Krikor and his companions were ordered to get off and line up at the rear. When Krikor turned the corner at the tailgate of the truck he started running across the open field. The other would be conscripts followed him. The soldiers opened fire and killed most of the men. The bodies of the Armenians were beheaded. The bloody heads were placed on poles in the middle of the village, a ghastly reminder of the power of the Turks over the remaining population. Krikor, the man who worked so hard in

Detroit to earn a living for his family, met his doom as a result of a murderous act. Vartouhi was devastated. She was left with a nine-months-old daughter and a four-year-old son.

The horrors of war are never greater than when inflicted on women and children. Children become the targets of irrational hate. Herod the King slew the male children in Bethlehem in an effort to kill the baby Jesus. Mary and Joseph were forewarned and took the child and fled into Egypt.

Vartouhi took her children and meager belongings and under cover of the darkness of night she headed for the seacoast. She was a devout Christian. Her prayers to Christ, her Savior, gave her the courage to flee for her life.

All the bridges and crossroads were guarded by soldiers. Their hatred of the Christian Armenians knew no bounds. Rape and other atrocities were committed against the women and children. The soldiers were merciless when faced with the screams and agony of the pitiful people. The stomachs of pregnant women were cut open. Fetuses were removed from the womb and impaled on the ends of swords and brandished for all to see.

The soldiers cursed and asked "Where is your God now?"

Vartouhi's prayers were answered. She was able to slip by the soldiers. After a harrowing journey she and her children reached the seacoast tired and hungry but otherwise unharmed.

She saw some Greek sailors and begged, "In the name of God please help me save my children."

The sailor were touched by her pleading and helped her escape. Vartouhi and her two children were successfully stowed away on a ship to Piraeus, Greece. They were quarantined for forty days.

After the quarantine was lifted four-year-old Sarkis went to work as a shoe black to help his mother eke out a living.

The seaport was a busy place with colorful sights and pungent smells. Ships from many parts of the world made it a port of call. Following a long sea voyage the sailors were eager to go on shore leave in Athens. Piraeus is the seaport for Athens. The sailors were the best customers for Sarkis' shoe blacking service. His tender years and ready smile struck a responsive chord in the hearts of the foreign seamen. The extra tips enabled Vartouhi to put more food on the table.

In spite of Sarkis' efforts in the shoe trade life became so difficult for the little family that Vartouhi had to return to the island of Cyprus. She had lived there with friends and relatives when Krikor worked in Detroit. She was there when he returned home.

On Cyprus, hard labor was the only recourse for the young widow and her children. Sarkis continued his work as a shoe black and Vartouhi took a job in a hosiery mill. The boy attended school sporadically. His work occupied most of his time. Sarkis' labor was harsh and he brushed elbows with the toughest street boys. Unlike Dickens' Oliver Twist, he didn't come under the influence of a Fagan or Artful Dodger. The dangers and adversities of early childhood forged a strong bond between Sarkis and his mother. Respect for her kept him on the proverbial straight and narrow path.

In his teenage years Sarkis found work as a laborer in a circus. One of his duties was to help set up a motorcycle act. The work was strenuous and was usually done late at night or early in the morning. The cyclists performed in a large steel lattice work globe. Their daring whirls around the sphere were a marvel of split second timing. To add to the excitement the motorcycles were operated with straight through exhaust pipes so they would make an earsplitting roar. The circus was popular and drew large crowds in the cities and towns of Cyprus. Sarkis was excited by the travel and the attention of the crowds.

While traveling with the circus Sarkis made friends with Garabed Shirinian in Nicosia, Cyprus. Garabed was an Armenian who had risen to become a foreman in the Cyprus Copper Mines, at Lefka. Garabed liked Sarkis and offered to help him get a job in the mines. This was a joint British/American business that was in steady operation during the 1930's.

Sarkis went to work in the Lefka mines. Garabed Shirinian was destined to play a far greater role in his life than that of supervisor toward one of his laborers. Garabed became a foreman in the mine through hard work. His personality was such that it made others want to work for him. They respected him because he never asked them to do something that he had not done or wouldn't do if such action were needed. A kind man, he would often take Sarkis to his home. He may have had an ulterior motive. He had four daughters and one son. One of the girls was named

Azadouhi which means liberty in English. Azadouhi and Sarkis were attracted to each other. Their meetings were chaperoned as was the custom in Cyprus in those days. Cupid's arrows lodged in their hearts in 1939 and they became engaged to be married.

In a colorful wedding ceremony in the Armenian Apostolic Church in Nicosia Garabed gave his daughter's hand in marriage to Sarkis. The wedding reception was held at Azadouhi's aunt's home.

Vartouhi sat quietly crying in a corner of the reception room. As she watched Sarkis laughing and hugging the guests she could see the physical features and personality that he had inherited from his father. Her bitter tears were in memory of Krikor. She blamed herself for his death at the hands of those vicious soldiers. It was she who persuaded him to return to Turkey. The terrible sight in the town square haunted her for the remainder of her life. In later years she was a fixture in the same pew every Sunday at the Armenian Apostolic Church in Larnaca, Cyprus. She said her prayers of thanksgiving for the life of her children. She believed that the hand of God led her on the dangerous roads of Turkey, guided her to Piraeus, Greece, sustained her through the difficult times in Greece and eventually led her to Cyprus where life was harsh but bearable. As a young widow with fierce self-reliance there were many men in her age group who would have been happy to take her as a wife. Vartouhi remained faithful to the memory of her dead husband and did not accept any of the proposals. The last years on Cyprus were the best years as she saw Sarkis and Sirarpi mature to raise families of their own. She died at the age of seventy and is buried in the graveyard near her church in Larnaca, a respected and revered member of the Yepremian family.

Chapter 3 &

In the NFL in 1939 the New York GIANTS defeat the Pro
All-Stars in the first Pro Bowl Game. The first NFL game
is televised from Ebbets Field, Brooklyn, between the
Brooklyn DODGERS and the Philadelphia EAGLES.

In far off Cyprus, Sarkis and Azadouhi's lives were
destined to be entwined in the future of the NFL.
The mysteries of life unwind into a pile of
happenings that defy the imagination. Azadouhi's
mother taught her how to be a seamstress. This
motivated Sarkis to start a business of his own. He
bought lumber and glass and built a mobile showcase
on a pushcart. He loaded the cart with colorful fabrics
and ready to wear items that Azadouhi made. His
muscles bulged and perspiration soaked through his
shirt as he pushed the cumbersome vehicle from
neighborhood to neighborhood. His labor in the
circus and in the Lefka mines prepared him for this
strenuous work. Sarkis was a salesman who told
stories and spread happiness wherever he traveled.

Cyprus was under British rule in 1939. Great Britain did all it could to prevent Jews from returning to Palestine where a revolution was brewing. Sarkis and his friends bought a small boat to engage in smuggling. The cargo often consisted of some highly motivated Jews who were willing to risk their lives to make their way to the promised land.

Sarkis considered this smuggling of human beings to be a humanitarian act. His father's death and the dispersion of his relatives and fellow Armenians to other parts of the world gave him a sense of kinship with the people who so desperately wanted to return to the land of their ancestors. Furthermore, the land was the well spring of his own religion. Also, the money he made was needed at home.

Sarkis' happiness was magnified when Azadouhi told him she was pregnant. His heart beat double time on August 2nd, 1940 when a son was born. They named him Krikor Sarkis Yepremian in honor of his grandfather. It is traditional in Armenian society to use the father's name as a middle name for a boy.

In the NFL in 1940 the clipping penalty is reduced from twenty-five yards to fifteen yards. The Pittsburgh team changes its name from the Pirates to the Steelers.
With the T-formation and man-in-motion the Chicago Bears defeat Washington 73-0 on December 8th in the Championship game.
Interest in Pro Football is increasing, Red Barber broadcasts the game over a 120-station lineup on the Mutual Broadcasting System.

Garabed Sarkis Yepremian followed Krikor into the world on June 2nd, 1944. The baby boy was named for his maternal grandfather, the mine foreman.

That year Ken Strong of the New York Giants attempted twelve field goals in the season and completed six of them. Green Bay defeats the New York Giants 14-7 in the NFL play-offs.

During the years of World War 2 there were tremendous shortages of food and other necessities on Cyprus. Sarkis would often bring fruit home to augment their skimpy meals. When Azadouhi bore her second son his overflowing joy filled the room. Azadouhi told him that he must go to see the doctor to give him the name of the baby.

Sarkis said, "I have taken care of that already. I named him Nazareth."

Azadouhi exclaimed, "No, no, we agreed to name him Garabed, my father's name."

Sarkis left the house to make the name change.

Later Sarkis came to see Azadouhi and said, "I have brought some fruit for you."

She said, "I don't want any fruit. I'm tired. I just want to rest."

Sarkis persisted, "Here take this fruit."

He pressed an object into the palm of her hand. She looked and saw that it was a British gold coin. Sarkis had bought it as a present for her. He was thrilled because she had presented him with another son.

Garabed was a contented child. Azadouhi nurtured him and proudly showed him to the neighbors. To her he was a beautiful baby. Privately, her friends thought he was an ugly boy. Pet names seem to be automatically bestowed on children. Garabed Sarkis Yepremian became known as little Garo.

The building in which they lived was two stories high. An older couple lived on the first floor. The Yepremians occupied the second floor. The old gentleman on the first floor was a respected hero in the neighborhood. He had volunteered for service in the Army in World War 1. People called him Gamavour which means volunteer. To add a little money to his veteran's pension he made colorful sugar candy birds on a stick. He spread them on a table in front of his house and offered the candy for sale. One day when four-year-old Garo was playing on the balcony above Gamavour's candy table the challenge to his boyhood was more than he could bear. Since time immemorial young boys have had contests to see who could pee the highest up the side of a building, or pole, or who could hit a knothole if one happened to be handy or hit any target of opportunity. Little Garo rose to the challenge. He whipped it out and aimed for the candy birds below. His aim was perfect. Garo sent a stream of pee across the row of birds. Old Gamavour exploded in rage.

He began to shout and curse in a loud voice, "I don't know why your mother brought you into the world. Why should I have to suffer because you are so bad?"

His yells caused Azadouhi to come running onto

the balcony. It didn't take her long to discover what had happened.

She said, "I'll buy sugar so you can replace the candy. I'm sure that Garo won't do that again."

After old Gamavour calmed down Azadouhi took Garo into the house and gave him a spanking and told him that he was forbidden to go out onto the balcony again.

There was another incident that emphasizes Garo's adventuresome nature. A political parade was staged in the streets of Larnaca with lots of music, flags, and general excitement. When the parade passed by Sarkis and Azadouhi were ready to go home Garo was nowhere to be found. They searched for him. No one had seen the boy. Sarkis remembered that after the parade ended there was to be a political rally in the town's auditorium. He went there to look for Garo. Sure enough, he was on the stage holding a flag. He had joined the marchers in the parade and wound up on the stage at the rally. Garo wanted to be in the middle of the action. He loved the center of attention. Little did he or anyone else know that fate had a lot of that in store for him in the future. Garo was not a bad boy but like most active youngsters he could be impish at times.

Father Mampre is a priest in the Armenian Apostolic church. Father Mampre's parents lived on the first floor of the house next door. During his visits home he would often talk to Garo. He told Garo that he should be a good boy and grow up to be a priest.

Garo said, "No, you wear too many clothes. It's too hot."

Father Mampre's heavy robes caused Garo to think that they would be too hot to wear.

Father Mampre answered, "It's not too hot. These clothes have fans hidden in them."

Such are the wonderful memories of childhood.

Genocide, poverty, hunger, hard labor and general turmoil caused deep-seated differences of political opinion among the Armenian people. When Krikor reached school age Sarkis and Azadouhi decided to send him to the American Academy in Larnaca rather than to the regular school. The Academy was founded by missionaries from a Presbyterian church in the Pittsburgh, Pennsylvania area. Krikor was a good student and an outstanding athlete. He was the school's tennis champion and captain of the field hockey team. This association with American teachers and his early readings about Dick, Jane and Sally had a profound effect on Krikor's future. He was fascinated by pictures from *LIFE, LOOK,* and the *SATURDAY EVENING POST.* His eventual migration to the United States changed the fortunes of the entire family.

When Garo reached school age it was decided that he would go to the Armenian school. Garo was a good student with a zest for life, a bright curiosity, and a keen anticipation of the school days ahead. He was able to concentrate for long periods when he wanted to solve a problem. Soccer players were the sports heroes on Cyprus. They were the glamour men and all of the young boys idolized them. Many of the boys dreamed of playing professional soccer when they grew up.

Garo was fortunate enough to get a soccer ball for a Christmas present. Before the Yepremians could afford to buy a regular soccer ball the boys would fold old socks together to make a ball. After their first soccer ball would no longer hold air they stuffed it with scraps of cloth from their mother's sewing table. The ball was heavier than a regular ball. Kicking the rag-stuffed ball developed Garo's leg strength. He became fascinated with the kicking game. During the warm summer months on Cyprus the stores closed and the people took a siesta between one and four p.m. Instead of taking a siesta Garo would go to the churchyard and kick his ball. There was a high wall around the church. He would kick the ball against the wall and retrieve it as it bounced back. Hour after hour with sweat drenching his body he would aim his kicks at spots on the wall. An occasional roach or grasshopper offered inviting targets. He was very good at breaking up lines of ants marching up the wall. Garo loved that wall. His imagination could turn it into a world famous soccer field where he was the star who scored the game winning goal. The wall became his friend. It reached out and told him to practice, practice, practice to gain his magic carpet ride to glory. The wall was his secret place of dreams. There, he could be the world famous star that people clamored to see. Often the nearby neighbors would be disturbed by the sound of the ball hitting the wall. When they complained too much Garo would go around to another side of the church and begin again.

One day the priest came from the church to complain to Azadouhi that Garo's kicking was making the church wall dirty. He wanted the kicking practice to stop.

Azadouhi, ever ready to defend her children, said, "Don't worry we will come and clean the wall."

Kicking was Garo's passion. When walking along the street any stray can was sure to be sent sailing away. Sometimes he would kick at small stones. Those stones were hard on his shoes and his parents would yell at him for treating his shoes so roughly.

In Larnaca, a trip to the shoemaker was a major event. Garo would get a new pair of shoes each year. The cobbler traced a line around each foot on a piece of cardboard. After cutting out the pattern he transferred the foot size to a piece of leather which was cut to become the sole of the shoe. The uppers were cut out and nailed to the sole. Primitive perhaps but the only shoes available at the time. They were a far cry from the high-tech athletic shoes of today. Garo was eleven-years-old before he owned a pair of shoes with cleats. Leather cleats were attached to the shoes by the local cobbler.

The playing of a professional soccer game in the town was a special event. Since he could not afford to buy tickets Krikor climbed a tree to see the game. As a usual custom children accompanied by their parents with tickets were admitted free. Garo waited at the gate. He saw a man and woman arriving without children. He darted out of the crowd and pretended to be with the couple. Garo pulled it off. He got in to see the game.

The summers were hot and dry on Cyprus. The grass on the soccer field was worn away and a thick layer of dust covered the playing area. Years later in England Garo saw his first soccer field with grass growing on it.

One day when Garo was in the sixth grade he came home with his report card. His mother noticed that he was trying to hide the card with his left hand.

She demanded, "Garo, let me see your report card."

In the marking system used in the Armenian school sixty was a passing grade. The highest grade on Garo's report card was fifty-nine and that was in physical education. She knew that Garo was very good in physical education. That was a signal to Azadouhi that her son was the victim of discrimination. Old political animosities were being directed toward Garo. She took him out of the Armenian school and enrolled him in the American Academy. Garo followed in the footsteps of his older brother. He was very competitive and worked to become a star athlete. He was an excellent tennis, field hockey and soccer player.

In 1956, Azadouhi bore another son. He was named Berj and became the family pet, the younger brother whom Krikor and Garo protected during his growing up years.

In September 1959 Krikor followed his dream and migrated to the United States.

He says, "For me it was America or bust."

Through the efforts of his Godfather he found an Armenian shoemaker in Evanston, Illinois who agreed to sponsor him. The ties of love and friendship created in the crucible of war and genocide tug at the heartstrings of the older generation of Armenians.

They want to help each other in the new world. Shortly after arriving in the United States Krikor enrolled at Indiana University. Sarkis and Azadouhi were building a new home in Larnaca, Cyprus-a home that they were never to occupy. They sold the house to get money to help Krikor at Indiana University. This charitable deed toward their first-born son was a key factor in the later fortunes of the Yepremian family. Krikor graduated in 1963.

In 1959 Lamar Hunt announced that he would form a second professional football league. The league would be called the American Football League. In 1960, Pete Rozelle is elected commissioner of the National Football League and the NFL awards the Dallas Cowboys a football franchise. The Minnesota Vikings are also added to the league that year.

Chapter 4 &

In 1960 economic conditions were bad on Cyprus. Internal unrest brought Sarkis' business to a standstill. The British soldiers were attacked by the Greeks. Car bombing and other war like acts were commonplace. The Turkish element on the Island of Cyprus was also in a state of unrest. Because of the hostilities many of Sarkis' customers were unable to pay for the merchandise he had delivered. In turn, he was unable to pay his suppliers for the goods he sold in the cloth trade.

There was real danger created by the shootings and bombings. Something had to be done. He decided to go to England to make a new life for his family. Since all Armenians are displaced persons the move was just another step in his desire to keep his family together.

After Sarkis left for England Azadouhi made arrangements to have the suppliers come to get their merchandise. Eventually everyone was paid. Sarkis cleared his debts.

Three months after his father went to England Garo decided to drop out of the Academy. He wanted to join his father in England.

Garo applied for his passport. He had to give his birth date. What a surprise. He was told that there was no record of a Garabed Sarkis Yepremian being born on June 2, 1944.

Garo said' "I know you are wrong. Here I am. I've been living for sixteen years."

The official searched the records again. He returned and repeated that there was no record of the birth of Garabed Sarkis Yepremian. He said there was a birth recorded on June 2nd, 1944. However, the name was Nazareth Yepremian. Suddenly, there was no longer a mystery. In his excitement over the birth of his second son Sarkis failed to change the name when Azadouhi insisted that he do so. Garo and his mother had to go through the process of an official name change. It took about two weeks to get the necessary paperwork approved. Finally, with passport in hand Garo was ready for his great adventure—another link in the chain of events that would lead him to greatness.

Garo exclaimed, "Wow! What excitement. I'm going to London to make my fortune."

He was booked to sail on a ship that was definitely not a luxury liner. There were about forty passengers housed on one lower deck. The bunks were arranged four high on each side of a curtained off space. These primitive and overcrowded rooms were hot and almost airless. The accumulated body odors caused people not to want to spend much time in them. The passengers ate the same food that was served to the crew. The first port of call was Beirut, Lebanon. Beirut was known as the Paris of the Middle East with bright lights and a wide-open atmosphere for tourist fun. A group of the male passengers asked Garo to lead them to a certain street in the city. The Greek and Turkish men didn't know the language. They were afraid to venture into the city without a guide. Garo could speak a little English and could find his way about.

When they arrived at their destination Garo noticed that there were a lot of neon signs displaying girls names. There was Lisa, Mary, Rose and other Americanized names. Garo and his group were in the "red light" district of Beirut. Garo is under the impression that the brothels were authorized by the government. He followed the older men up a flight of stairs to a second floor room where several girls were lounging about in see-through nighties. The smell of perfume floated on the air. The men began to negotiate with the women. Garo almost went into a state of shock. At the age of sixteen he had been reared in a society where dating was practically unknown. Boy and girl meetings were mostly chaperoned affairs after proper introductions by the parents. To say the least, he had kept his sex life well in hand up to this point. This wide-open city with colorful signs and amorous ladies was a frightening place. He ran like a scared rabbit. He could hear the women laughing as he went down the stairs and into the noisy street where he waited for the men he was guiding.

Garo says, "I had thirteen English pounds in my pocket. That is equivalent to twenty-six American dollars. I had to make that money last until I got to London."

After the adventure in Beirut Garo didn't want to stray far from the ship. Some passengers left the ship in Beirut and were replaced by other travelers.

Among the new passengers there were a classical guitar player and a French family with a sixteen-year-old daughter. The ship left Beirut and headed for Port Said, Egypt. The classical guitar player made a play for the French girl. He was accustomed to receiving a lot of attention because of his talent. He thought that the girl would fall in love with him. Much to his surprise the young lady seemed to prefer the company of Garo. She and Garo held hands and walked on the deck in the moonlight. She couldn't speak Greek or English and Garo couldn't speak French. They had a minor shipboard romance in spite of the language difficulty. However, the affair did not progress beyond the hand holding stage.

After Port Said, the next stop was at Alexandria, Egypt. From there the ship sailed to Piraeus, Greece. During this time Garo's innocent puppy love affair with the French girl continued. In Piraeus they were able to leave the ship and get some decent food. It was a break from the humble fare served on board. They left Piraeus and sailed through the Corinth Canal and headed for Naples, Italy. They were warned to look out for bandits in Naples. From Naples their next stop was Genoa, Italy. The strange architecture fascinated Garo. It was certainly different from the strictly utilitarian buildings on Cyprus. Marseilles, France was the final destination. Garo was bedeviled by the fear that the boat would leave port without him. He was usually on the ship three or four hours before sailing time.

Garo also developed another troubling worry. The male Greek passengers that he guided in Beirut told Garo that the parents of the French girl were going to force him to marry her when they got to France. Garo was naive. He didn't have any spare money and he had to meet his father in London.

Worry! Worry! Worry! Sure enough. When they arrived in Marseilles the girl's father invited Garo to go home with them for a few days. Garo liked the girl but wasn't ready for marriage.

He shouted, "No, no, I must go to London to meet my father."

He ran toward the train station to begin the next leg of his journey. The Greeks were much amused by the false fears they created for Garo. He was an unsophisticated Cyprus boy venturing forth into the world for the first time. Garo got on the train for the overnight trip to Paris. He walked into a compartment that had four seats on each side. He sat in the only empty seat. To his dismay, a familiar Turkish man was in the next seat. The fellow was wearing the same clothing he had worn since the start of the voyage from Cyprus. Garo remembers the khaki shorts, brown socks and yellow shirt and the transistor radio on the man's shoulder. The man thought he was "cool."

The train departed and everyone tried to get comfortable. The Turk took his shoes off. Garo has smelled some strong cheese during his lifetime. However, this was worse than the smelliest goat cheese in the whole wide world. Garo withstood the odor for about an hour. He retreated to the corridor next to the compartment and sat on his suitcase until the train arrived in Paris. In Paris he found another compartment for the trip to Boulougne, France. At Boulougne he left the train and went directly to the ferry to cross the English Channel to Dover. The channel waters were rough and many people got seasick on the crossing. Garo stayed on deck in the cold air and was able to avoid motion sickness. At Dover he boarded another train bound for Victoria station.

At Victoria station there were some moments of panic. With all of the worries about money, worries about a forced marriage, and the uncertainty of a new life, Garo had lost weight during the thirteen-day trip from Cyprus. He had not seen his father in three months and the station was packed with people. After about five minutes that seemed to Garo to be five hours Sarkis located him and they had a happy reunion. Sarkis hailed a cab and Garo took his first ride in a British taxi. They wound through the dark and rainy streets with the windshield wipers running. Garo began to think that London wasn't so great after all. Ever the optimist, he had imagined that his father would be living in a fine home in a nice part of the city. His impressions of London came from movies that he had seen on Cyprus. They arrived at a group of row houses on a narrow side street. Sarkis paid the cab driver and led the way to a basement door. They walked down the steps and entered what was to be Garo's new home.

The basement room had a kitchen on one side and two beds on the other side. Garo was tired after his travels. He had no trouble sleeping in the run down apartment. The next day Sarkis made his usual rounds looking for work. His English was not good therefore, he went to the Greek and Turkish communities because he felt comfortable there. He frequented the coffee shops to talk about work opportunities.

On the second day of his London stay Garo found an old record player in the basement apartment. There was only one record and that was Tony Bennett's *IN THE MIDDLE OF AN ISLAND*. The player wouldn't work because it didn't have a needle in the sound cartridge. Garo had no money to buy another needle. He found a straight pin and put it in the cartridge and, wonder of wonders, the record player worked. Garo played that song over and over until he knew every word and every note. To this day he is a big Tony Bennett fan. Garo wanted to be a singer. He practiced every day.

Garo quickly learned that the single bathroom on the second floor had to serve all of the people who lived in the building. There were no exhaust fans. The bathroom floor was littered with matches that people had burned to take out the offensive odors. The shower had a water meter on it. A threepenny coin would provide about five minute worth of hot water.

Garo stayed in that basement apartment everyday for about a month. The isolation was difficult. He was accustomed to talking to many friends, schoolmates and neighbors on Cyprus. After Sarkis left the apartment in the morning Garo would clean the breakfast dishes and make up the beds. It was a chore to pass the time away. He would pretend to be a famous kicker on a soccer team. A roll of socks wound over a crumpled newspaper was his ball. He practiced by kicking it at cracks in the wallpaper. In those dismal apartments they didn't strip the wallpaper before applying a new layer. The new paper went on right over the old. Because of the wet weather in London the wallpaper was often damp and soggy. Many cracks and tears showed. Kicking a rolled up sock-er ball at the wall didn't do much damage. It was a game to Garo and helped keep his leg muscles warmed up.

There were a number of people who walked their dogs past Garo's basement apartment window. He was starved for conversation and feeling lonely during those long days of idleness. He bounded up the stairs to the sidewalk and struck up conversations with the dog walkers. He made friends with an old gentleman who was retired from the British Navy. The man was eager to talk. He was suffering from the loneliness of retirement and found Garo to be a welcome diversion. Garo learned a lot about London during those friendly conversations. Picadilly Circus, London Bridge and Hyde Park were places he was eager to visit.

Six weeks after Garo arrived in London, Azadouhi and younger brother Berj made the trip from Cyprus. They came on the same boat, train, ferry route that Garo had taken earlier. The family was reunited in the basement apartment.

Shortly after she arrived in London, Azadouhi found a job in a factory that made tunics for the Palace Guard. Garo got a job in the same factory as a fabric cutter. After they received a paycheck they arranged to move to a better apartment on the third floor in the same building. It had a couple of rooms and a real kitchen. Sarkis' contacts within the Armenian community helped him find a location where he opened a coffee shop. Later, the Yepremians moved into an apartment at 16 Essex Road, The Angel, Islington, North London. The apartment was on the second floor and had its own bathroom. A laundromat located beneath the apartment helped heat the apartment in the winter. However, in the summer the heat from the laundromat was very uncomfortable. There was another disadvantage. The draperies were kept closed on the street side windows. The passengers on the second deck of the passing double decker busses could look right into the Yepremian's living quarters.

Garo worked in the tunic factory for two years. When he was seventeen years old he bought a Ford Anglia. He loved that car. He washed it so often that his friends said it was better than new. Prior to buying the car he wanted to buy a motorcycle.

His father said, "You buy a motorcycle and I'll break both of your legs."

Perhaps Sarkis remembered the daring motorcycle riders from his circus days. He was afraid that Garo would be killed riding a motorcycle. Sarkis gave Garo the down payment for the Ford Anglia. Garo immediately developed automobile fever. Automobiles have been his passion ever since that first experience with the Anglia.

Garo played soccer on the weekends. He played for the Turkish team at Hackney Marshes on Saturday and with an Armenian team at Chiswick on Sunday. He

was a good player and was a much sought after team
member. The players got into uniform at home and
drove to the game. After the game they'd drive home
and get out of the uniform. There were no locker
rooms for these amateur players.

In 1962 a friend of Sarkis' wanted to open a restaurant in Manchester, England. He needed someone
dependable to run his fabric shop in Soho. The man
knew that Garo was a reliable worker. He hired Garo
to help his son run the shop. Garo was paid seven
pounds sterling per week for six days work. Selling
fabrics to the wholesale trade was the main business of
the shop. Many of the customers were foreigners.
Garo learned a lot of simple math, percentages,
multiplication, addition etc. He also learned how to
change foreign money into British money and vice
versa. He worked in that business until 1966.

*In the NFL in 1966 the goal posts are standardized with
uprights twenty feet above the cross bar. The rights for the
Super Bowl telecast are sold to NBC and CBS for
9.5 million dollars. New Orleans is awarded an NFL
franchise. The American public is in love with the game of
football and fans are eager to root for the home team.*

Chapter 5 ❧

That mystical chain of fate is ready to pull Garo another step along the road of destiny. Krikor, Garo's brother graduated from Indiana University in 1963. He went on to law school for one year. He married Markanna Fry and became the father of a son. They named him Sarkis. In the Armenian tradition they called him Sarko for short.

Krikor came to visit his parents and brothers in London in 1966. Markanna wanted to see the famous landmarks of London. Krikor was anxious for his son to be baptized at St. Sarkis, the Armenian church on High Street in the Kensington district of London. There was a dark cloud hanging over Krikor's life. He felt guilty because he had been able to go to college with the financial help of his parents while Garo had to drop out of high school when times got rough and civil war threatened to break out on Cyprus in 1960.

In the United States Krikor had seen Pete and Charlie Gogolak kick a football, soccer style, in Ivy League games. He thought that Garo might become a good football kicker. He hadn't seen Garo kick in seven years and wondered if he could still kick the ball. On one of the sightseeing trips the Yepremians visited Stratford-on-Avon and Windsor Castle. Garo and Krikor talked about American style football. They decided to buy an American football to see if Garo could kick the oval pigskin. They looked in several sporting goods shops but were unable to find an American football. Instead, they drove to a nearby park where Krikor asked Garo to kick the soccer ball as far and as high as he could. Garo showed Krikor that he was a strong and accurate soccer kicker. Krikor was elated.

He said to Garo, "You've got to come to America. You can get a free education."

Garo was skeptical about receiving a free education for kicking a football.

He says, "I didn't want to leave London. I thought I had a good job. I could afford to have an automobile and my friends were in London."

Garo's dreams of becoming a famous soccer player were fading fast. The law in England at that time said that you had to be born in England to play in the English soccer leagues. That's why Garo was playing with the Turkish and Armenian teams on the weekends. He thought that his real future was in sales in the fabric business. Maybe, some day he might get a higher position in the company. Also, Garo didn't think that his Mom would let him go. By the way, he still listens to his Mom.

His mother said, "Go. If you like it stay. If you don't like it come back."

It was decided that he would go to the United States to take advantage of the free education that Krikor said was his for the asking.

Garo thought, "Krikor must be rich. Krikor must have married a very rich woman. After all he was able to travel to England for a visit."

Krikor offered to pay Garo's way to the United States. As a further test, Garo asked him what kind of car he owned in America. When Krikor said that he owned a Chevrolet that was the clincher. In England if you owned a Chevrolet you were considered to be "in the money."

Garo reasoned, "If I try out for a football scholarship in America and don't make it Krikor will surely help me get back to England."

Garo had never been in an airplane before and he was terrified to fly over the Atlantic ocean. He went to London's Heathrow airport where a friend of his worked. Garo watched the large planes take off and land. His friend assured him that it would be safe and that the stewardesses would guide him on the journey.

Soon a letter arrived from Krikor with Garo's ticket along with a letter of instructions. Garo was told that he would land at the International Terminal at Kennedy airport in New York. A limousine would transfer him and his baggage to the domestic terminal for the flight to Indianapolis.

"Wow" said Garo, "My brother must be really rich if he can afford to rent a limousine for me."

To Garo the word limousine meant that a Bentley or Rolls Royce would be there to take him from one terminal to another.

When Garo got on the plane he had a suitcase in his

hand and a guitar slung over his shoulder. He thought his long sideburns, jeans, and guitar would make him look important in the United States. Elvis Presley was one of his favorite Americans. His knowledge of the United States was mainly gained by watching movies made in the States. He also was carrying a paper bag filled with an Armenian treat called Lahmajoun. They are round like a small pizza. Garo's mom knew that Krikor loved them. She made Garo promise to deliver them to Krikor. When he arrived at the International terminal in New York the customs officers asked if he was carrying any food items.

"Yes."

He pointed out that his Mom had given him the Lahmajoun to bring to his brother. The customs people would not allow him to bring the food items into the country. They were tossed into the garbage. Garo followed the directions given in Krikor's letter. He went outside and looked for the luxury limo he thought would be there to greet him. After sitting on his suitcase for forty-five minutes he began to get nervous. He went inside to the information desk and in his best broken English he asked the attendant about the limo service. She directed him to a long Pontiac vehicle that didn't look so plush to him.

He mused, "My brother must not be as rich as I thought."

He rushed to the limo and was able to make his connecting flight to Indianapolis. The plane made several stops.

At each landing Garo would jump up and ask the stewardess "Is this Indianapolis?"

The flight attendant knew he was nervous. She told

him that she would make sure that he got off at the right airport.

Krikor was there to meet Garo at the flight gate. After a happy reunion they went to the parking lot and got into Krikor's car. Garo made a mental note of the '65 Chevy Nova's condition. It was a stick shift, had no radio and no air conditioning. It was a stripped down model.

"He's not so rich after all," thought Garo.

They arrived at Krikor's apartment. It was located in the basement of a three story building. It reminded Garo that his first home in London was in a basement. There was a big difference. This was a very nice apartment. Krikor and Markanna set up a bed for Garo in the baby's room. The baby crib was moved into the living room.

That evening, they went out to celebrate Garo's safe arrival. They dined in high style at Howard Johnson's. Garo ordered fried clams and thought they were wonderful. He was overwhelmed by the wide variety of ice cream flavors on the dessert menu. What a wonderful country...so many ice cream flavors. That first week he had a meal of Kentucky Fried Chicken.

Garo says, "It was the most wonderful chicken I had ever eaten. To this day I love Kentucky Fried Chicken."

Krikor bought a football and a tee. The next evening, they went to a nearby practice field at Butler University. It was the only available field with goal posts. They began the practice with Garo kicking off from the tee. Garo had the leg strength to kick the ball a long way. His kickoffs were long enough to go into the end zone of a regulation field. They switched to field goal practice. Garo couldn't kick the oval football high enough to get it over the crossbar on the goal posts. His instinct was to kick the ball low and into a soccer goal net.

In his mind, Krikor was rapidly losing faith in his dreams of a free education for brother Garo. He tried to hide his disappointment. He knew that college kickers served years of apprenticeship in high school football. He thought his early optimism about Garo may have been more hope than reality.

Some people accept defeat early in their battle to attain a goal. Others reach inside their beings and find the strength to continue the fight. Like a gunfighter out of the old west, Garo had a quick burning fire blazing deep down inside that made his eyes and muscles spring alert with hair-trigger expectancy. He couldn't disappoint his brother, his family, and his friends who had faith in his ability to become a good football kicker.

A football kick looks like a simple event. However, it is deceptive. The slightest misalignment of foot against ball causes a deflection that is magnified by the long flight to the goal.

That night Garo lies awake in bed perspiring in the intense summer heat. He agonizes about his kicking problem. In that moment when the brain is neither awake nor asleep Garo's imagination is so vivid it becomes an out-of-body experience. He is on the practice field. Suddenly, his disembodied spirit takes him to the center of the field. As he looks toward the sideline he sees a still life scene as if in a technicolor movie. He sees himself getting set to kick. Krikor is on the left side holding his forefinger on the tip of the

football. His brother has a sad look on his face. Markanna and little Sarko are there on the sideline. Behind
them stands a great crowd of the living and the dead.
His Mother and Father are there and behind them he
can see his long-dead Grandfather and Grandmother
Vartouhi and Garabed the mine foreman. There are
uncountable numbers of others he perceives to be the
displaced Armenians of history. The field glows with a
delicate radiant energy from an almighty power.

Garo's parents taught him to have faith in God. His
boyhood memories are filled with family legends
about his Grandmother and Father's flight from
Turkey and the poverty and hard work endured by his
parents and grandparents as they made their way in the
world. The elements of character are planted in the
mind of a child who then carries them into adulthood.

The scene sprang to life, Garo hears the people
murmuring words of encouragement. He is aware of
the aroma in the air. It smells like well-seasoned oak
burning in a fireplace with oil of roses mixed with the
smoke. It is a comfortable feeling of being at peace
with the world. He watches himself run up to the ball.
He sees that his steps in the approach are all wrong.
His left leg swings in its accustomed arc. His foot hit
the ball too near the center which makes it fly away
close to the ground. He knows that he must plant his
right foot a little closer to the ball. The right foot
works as an anchor for his left leg swing. Krikor
retrieves the ball. Once again he kneels to hold it for a
field goal try. Garo sees himself move a little closer to
the ball and take slightly shorter steps. His right foot
comes down a few inches nearer the target. His head
and shoulders thrust forward and his powerful left leg

swings in a graceful arc—a vision of perfect kicking technique. The football soars over the bar in the center of the goal posts. The faces in the crowd are filled with joy. Their thunderous shouts echo from the hilltops. He sees himself leap in victory. And then, the colors of the scene dim and the sounds fade away. Garo is asleep.

The next morning Krikor and Markanna are surprised at Garo's exuberance and high spirits. He is in a jolly mood. He pretends to pick a guitar and swings his hips as he sings, "One for the money, two for the show, three to get ready, go kick go."

It is his parody of Elvis Presley singing *DON'T STEP ON MY BLUE SUEDE SHOES*. At that evening's practice session, much to Krikor's surprise, Garo sends the ball over the crossbar with amazing regularity. His dreams for Garo came back in full force.

Chapter 6 ❧

Garo had an international driver's license. His daily routine was to eat breakfast and drive Markanna to her job at the hospital where she worked as a medical technologist. He would drop Krikor off at Block's department store where he was an assistant to the vice president. With his one-year-old nephew, Sarko, in the back seat of the Chevy Nova he returned home and took care of the baby.

During those long hours in the apartment he watched television sitcoms and soap operas. He learned a lot about life in the United States from those television shows. Some of his ideas about this country weren't realistic but at least it was a start. About 2:00 P.M. he drove to the hospital and picked up his sister-in-law and came home for a couple of hours rest. After that he drove into downtown Indianapolis to pick up Krikor at the department store.

Krikor was a man of the world and seemed to know everybody. One evening when they were going to the practice field they saw Jack Benny at the back door of the university's theater. He was there for one of his comedy show appearances. Garo knew that Jack Benny was a big time star.

Krikor yelled, "Hi Jack."

Jack waved back and replied, "Hi buddy."

Garo was impressed. He thought, "Wow, my brother really does know a lot of people."

Krikor was proud of his brother. He bragged to his co-workers that Garo was going to become a famous football player. When they met Garo they thought Krikor was nuts. They expected to see a big man. What they saw was a skinny, balding, five-foot-seven-inch kid.

Practice, practice, practice. Within a few weeks Garo split the uprights regularly from 50 and 55 yards away.

Tony Hinkle, the coach of the Butler University Bulldogs, came riding by on a bicycle. He saw one of the long kicks and darn near flipped over the handle bars. He couldn't believe his eyes. Tony came over and began to talk to the boys.

He spoke to Garo, "I want you to enroll in Butler University."

Garo was not fluent in English.

He said, "Talk to my brother."

Tony told Krikor, "Have your brother enroll tomorrow. We can give him a partial scholarship."

Krikor replied, "My brother can't make it on a partial scholarship."

Tony said, "Go tomorrow and register as a music major."

Garo interjected, "What does he mean-music major?"

Krikor spoke to Garo in Armenian, "Don't worry the dean of music is a football fanatic. Perhaps he can be of some help."

Tony with more urgency in his voice, "Just go register. We'll find some people from the city who will sponsor you."

He was anxious to get this kicking phenom into his football program.

The next day Garo showed up at the registrar's office. It quickly became apparent that he could not meet the academic standards to be enrolled in the university. Garo had dropped out of the Academy on Cyprus in 1960 before completing his senior year.

The school officials had a consultation and offered to let Garo go to class as an audit student. That would give him an opportunity to pass his high school equivalency examination and be enrolled as a regular student.

Bill Sylvester, the assistant coach of the Butler Bulldogs who worked with the freshman team, told Garo he would be unable to practice with the regular players because he was not yet a full fledged college student.

They gave Garo a counselor's room. By the way, he was the only student who had a phone in his room. He was issued meal tickets and provided with a tutor. The coaches were anxious for him to make the team. Garo was outfitted with a tee shirt and a pair of shorts. He practiced on his own initiative. Each day at practice time he would go out and concentrate on kicking.

Garo became somewhat of a celebrity. Most of the

fraternities were rushing him in anticipation of his becoming a big football star.

An article in a local newspaper sums it up rather nicely.

GARO YEPREMIAN OF CYPRUS CAN BOOT 'EM A MILE

BY CORKEY LAMM

Butler football coach Tony Hinkle has a man from Cyprus on his freshman squad, a "walk on" music student who might turn out to be the most exciting player ever to pull on a blue jersey.

He's 22-year-old Garo Sarkis Yepremian, who speaks four languages-his native Armenian, Greek, Turkish and English-but his talking point is his left foot.

A soccer player, Garo kicks field goals.

Zounds! How he kicks them.

He has been kicking field goals under the watchful eye of his brother Krikor, a 26-year-old graduate of Indiana University and captain of the Hoosiers' 1963 soccer team. He has been doing it for two months. And the crowds gather.

Krikor flat out says, "He better than the Gogalaks."

Now the Gogalaks-Pete, with the New York Giants and Charley with the Washington Redskins, are a couple of Hungarian brothers whose soccer-type kicks livened things up for Cornell and Princeton these past few years.

An inspection of Garo's left-footed wizardry will make any connoisseur of kicking gasp.

Garo doesn't even have a high school diploma which is one reason he's on "special student" status at Butler signed up to study piano, voice and physical education.

"If he demonstrates he can carry university work," said assistant coach Bill Sylvester who recruited him, "then he can be accepted as a student working toward a degree."

The missing educational links, Garo explains in understatement, were caused by the turmoil between Greeks and Turks on Cyprus.

"There was some trouble there," he says.

Another newspaper writer added the following article:

MUSIC MAJOR KICKS FOR BUTLER

BY BOB PIERCE

It takes more to please a football crowd than tearing up turf and cracking shoulder pads.

The star, the crowd pleaser, has that quality of individuality that makes him stand out in a field of bodies in motion. Such a player can be found every afternoon on Butler's football field.

His name is Garo Sarkis Yepremian, a 22-year-old music major with the potential to send a star's electrifying spark through a crowd who can barely pronounce his name.

The articles were published in the local papers after a scrimmage between the Butler freshman and varsity teams.

Coach Bill Sylvester said, "This will be an unofficial event. You may have an opportunity to make a kick for an extra point."

Garo asked, "What do you mean extra point."

Coach Sylvester had to explain it to him.

The fans were surprised when they saw Garo. He did not wear any pads under his uniform shirt. He kicked off and the ball sailed through the opposing end zone. His first field goal try was from 48 yards out. The ball traveled under the crossbar 12 inches short. Krikor was quite angry over the call. He and some other fans said the ball actually went over the crossbar. Later in the game the freshmen team scored a touchdown. Garo came in for the extra point attempt. He kicked the ball through the uprights high over the bar. The ball sailed out of the stadium and landed on the nearby university theater roof.

Coach Tony Hinkle said he was as good or better than Butler's greatest kicker.

For the next three weeks Garo was unable to practice with the team.

The coach called him in and said, "I have good news and bad news for you. Under the NCAA rules you cannot play college football. You are 22-years-old and your class has graduated. You also played soccer for four years in England. Athletes are only allowed to play one sport at a time. The good news is that the people who sponsored you have been pleased with you and are willing to continue your sponsorship for four years."

Garo said, "I've got to talk to my brother."

When Garo saw Krikor he said, "Don't worry about it. I have other plans for you."

Prior to coach Sylvester's news about Garo's ineligibility for college football a local reporter came out to the practice field to do a story about Garo. The reporter asked Garo to do some kickoffs for the accompanying photographer. The photog took several shots. For one of the pictures he placed his camera at ground level. Garo looked like he might be at least six-feet-six inches tall from that angle. Simple things in life sometimes bring the greatest rewards. That picture played a pivotal role in the chain of circumstances driving Garo to his destiny.

Chapter 7 🐚

Krikor is a man of dreams. He doesn't give up his dreams at the first sign of failure. Krikor prepared a letter telling about Garo's kicking prowess. He included a copy of the low angle picture and a copy of a newspaper article that told about Garo making 19 out of 20 field goal attempts from 50 yards out. He sent a copy of the letter, the picture and the newspaper article to twenty pro teams.

"I didn't write to Washington or the New York GIANTS. That's where the Gogalak brothers play," said Krikor. "I didn't write to Minnesota because I didn't know the correct address. I wrote to every other team in the AFL and NFL."

The Atlanta FALCONS and The Detroit LIONS called the same day they received the letter. Later letters came in from Houston, St. Louis, Baltimore and Green Bay.

The FALCONS called first. Krikor agreed to come to Atlanta for a tryout. Thirty minutes later the

Detroit LIONS office called. They wanted to give Garo a tryout.

They said, "What is a good day?"

Krikor said, "Thursday."

The FALCONS sent a ticket to Garo and he and Krikor flew to Atlanta on Tuesday, October 12th, 1966. Garo was still very nervous about flying. Krikor booked a room across from Atlanta's Fulton County Stadium. Garo went to sleep at 8:30. Now it was Krikor's time to be nervous. He couldn't sleep. Worry, worry, worry. He awakened Garo at 8:00am. Garo was annoyed and wanted to stay in bed.

Krikor said, "The tryout is at ten o'clock. You can't stay in bed. You have to loosen up and be ready."

Garo said, "I'm hungry. Can we have something to eat?

After a very light breakfast Krikor made Garo walk all the way around the stadium. They went to the players entrance. Garo told the security guard that he was to tryout for the football team.

The guard looked and saw this 142-pound nearly bald-headed young man and said, "Oh, you want the soccer team. It's down the road about a mile-and-a-half."

Garo replied, "No, I want the football team. I have a tryout."

Krikor chimed in and confirmed that Garo was there for a tryout.

While the discussion with the security guard was taking place, Rankin Smith, the owner of the FALCONS, said to Krikor, "You must be Garo."

Krikor said, "No, that's Garo,"

He pointed toward his brother.

Rankin blurted out, "My God we spent a lot of money to bring you here. I guess we might as well look at you."

He was disappointed. His team was winless in five games since he bought the new franchise. The week before the team was holding its own against the REDSKINS until Charlie Gogolak, the REDSKINS soccer style kicker, connected for two field goals in the third quarter. When the picture and story about Garo came to Atlanta he and coach Norb Hecker were excited and called Indianapolis right away.

Garo was taken into the locker room. The equipment man thought this was going to be some kind of joke. He gave Garo a large sweat suit. The shirt hung down to his knees. Garo tucked the shirt inside of the pants and pulled the pants up under his arms. He used his own well worn shoes. He and Krikor went on to the field. The head coach, Norb Hecker, was nowhere in sight.

Garo warmed up by starting with 30-yard kicks. He progressed to 35 yards and then on to 40-yards. A couple of players began to notice this little balding fellow as he kicked the ball through the uprights after approaching the ball from a strange angle. When he put a 50-yarder through the goal posts Bobby Etter the player who had been designated to kick field goals for the Falcons got very excited.

He ran into the clubhouse and said to Norb Hecker, "Hey, coach! You better to come out here and see this little guy kick the football."

Hecker went onto the field and watched Garo kick.

When Garo put one through the uprights from 55 yards Hecker said, "You're doing very well without any pressure. Let's see what you can do with pressure."

Garo didn't understand what Hecker meant.

He said to Krikor in Armenian, "What does he mean pressure? Does he want to put more air in the ball?"

The next thing Garo saw was a bunch of huge players dashing out to take up positions in front and around himself. He had never seen that many large men before in his entire life. He wondered where they got all of them. Their football pads made them look even larger than life.

The players lined up and the ball was snapped. There followed an unbelievable demonstration. From 55 yards Garo made 18 out of 20 attempts with the defensive team rushing as in almost game conditions.

The last kick hit the cross bar and bounced away.

Garo apologized and said, "I must be getting a little tired."

Coach Hecker called for a golf cart and said, "Let's go into the office."

Garo said, "I can walk."

Norbert Hecker graduated from Baldwin-Wallace college and played end with the Los Angeles RAMS from 1951 to 1953. He then moved on and completed his professional career with the Washington REDSKINS from 1955 to 1957. Norbert Hecker was a tested veteran in the violent world of pro football. He was not easily impressed.

In response to Garo's offer to walk Hecker replied, "You may never have to walk again."

They went by the office secretary. She giggled when she saw Garo perspiring in his oversized sweat suit with the pants pulled up under his arms. She thought

Garo was a comedian who was going to be part of a half time show.

As the negotiation got underway, Rankin Smith offered $13,000 and a one-year contract. Garo had been making $26.00 per week in England and this seemed like a fortune to him.

He spoke to Krikor in Armenian and said, "Let's go ahead and sign."

Krikor replied, "Are you crazy. We've got a fish on the hook here."

He turned and said to Rankin, "Look, we have a tryout with Detroit tomorrow. That's why we can't give you an answer today."

While they were being shown out Rankin Smith said, "Will you change your mind if I throw in a new car?"

Before leaving England to come to the United States Garo told his friends he was going to go to the United States to be a success and buy a new Ford Mustang car. When Rankin Smith said he would throw in a new car Garo saw his dreams coming to pass in miraculous fashion. He and Krikor had a big argument in Armenian. Garo insisted that he should sign right now, on the spot. He wanted his Mustang. Krikor's logic prevailed even though the argument continued all the way to the airport. When the flight started they felt like winners. Krikor's dreams were coming true. They were sure of a contract.

The plane hit some turbulence on the way home. Garo prayed to God for safety.

He pleaded, "Dear Lord, this is my first chance. Please don't take it away from me."

When the brothers arrived home they were happy.

They felt triumphant. They picked up Markanna and little Sarko and took a flight to Detroit. That evening they went to the Howard Johnson motel near TIGER stadium. The motel was fully booked. The room clerk was able to find them a single room with a roll away cot. Garo had no trouble going to sleep. Krikor was very nervous.

The next day they went to the Detroit LIONS office and met Russ Thomas, the General Manager. He was surprised to see them.

He said, "Why are you here? You signed with Atlanta."

A writer who was on the field at Fulton County Stadium when Garo had his tryout wrote an article praising the kicking exhibition and it was put on the Associated Press wire to all parts of the country. Russ had assumed that Garo had been signed by the FALCONS.

They went on the field. Garo was met with respect by the LIONS. Most of the team was on the field to see this phenomenal kicker they had read about in the newspapers.

Garo went through his kicking routine and began to split the uprights from 55-yards.

Alex Karras, Detroit's star defensive lineman yelled, "Sign him up. Don't wait. Get the paper. Sign him right now, right here on the field."

The players burst into a spontaneous round of applause for what they had seen this man do.

Wayne Walker who had been handling the place kicking for the Lions said, "He's the best kicker I've ever seen."

Head Coach Harry Gilmer, ex-quarterback for the

Washington REDSKINS and former assistant coach of the Minnesota VIKINGS, said to Russ Thomas, "I want this boy for the Sunday game. Do whatever you have to do to get him."

Krikor's, eyes lit up. After Garo took a shower they went to Russ Thomas' office. William Clay Ford, grandson of Henry Ford and owner of the team, came into the room and was introduced. When Garo heard the name he was impressed. He felt close to his Mustang dream. Lee Iacocca and the Ford Motor Company had brought the Mustang to market in mid-year 1964.

Mr. Ford offered Garo a two-year deal at $20,000. per year.

He said, "If you will sign today we'll give you a $10,000. signing bonus."

Krikor said, "We'd like to go to lunch and then we'll come back."

After they left the stadium office Garo said to Krikor, "Are you crazy?"

As soon as they got back to the motel Krikor got on the phone and called the FALCONS and talked to Norb Hecker.

Krikor said, "My brother wants to come to Atlanta if you can match his offer from the Lions."

Norb asked,"How much is it?

Krikor told him it was $35,000. the first year and $35,000 the second year with a $25,000 signing bonus. Norb was shocked.

He said, "We aren't even paying our first round draft choice that much."

Tommy Nobis, a middle linebacker was the draft choice he was talking about.

Norb continued, "We can't match the offer" and hung up the phone.

Krikor reminded Garo that he did not have a working permit.

Krikor said, "We'll make the LIONS help us get the papers. The second condition is that I come to Detroit and work for the Ford Motor Company."

After lunch they went back to the LIONS office and Krikor said, "We have no problem with the contract however, there is one condition. I need a job in Detroit."

Mr. Ford replied, "With your talents I want you in our customer relations department."

They proceeded to write out a check to Garo for $10,000 and told him to go to Indianapolis get his belongings and return to Detroit the next day. Ford asked him what number he wanted on his jersey.

Garo said, "Give me number 1. It fits my chest and not only that I want to be number one."

Garo came back to Detroit the next day with his old battered suitcase and guitar. He was met at the airport by two attorneys who put him in a limo and went to get his papers in order. They took him to the police station to be finger printed and to the Social Security office to get his number followed by a trip to the immigration office. By 8:00 P.M. Garo's paperwork was finished. The attorneys checked him into the Leland House hotel, a very nice place. The next morning, which was Saturday, offensive guard Bob Kowalkowski and offensive tackle Doug Van Horn came to pick him up. They arrived in a sting ray chevy Corvette. Garo scrunched up in the rear seat and rode to the airport. The team boarded the plane for the trip to Baltimore.

Improbable as it sounds Garo Yepremian who had never seen a real football game, except on television, was going to play in an NFL pro game.

Krikor went on to work for the Ford Motor Company for four years. He knew nothing about automobiles from a technical standpoint. He was very good at pacifying disgruntled customers. He made sure that they were put in touch with the appropriate district manager who would then solve the customer's problem.

When Krikor first wrote the letters to the NFL teams his wife, Markanna, said, "Who the hell do you think you are to write to those teams?"

She and Krikor had a big argument. Their marital difficulties eventually culminated in divorce.

At Butler University, the mood was sad. Everyone was sorry that Garo could not be enrolled and made eligible to play football there.

Richard Dickinson, Assistant Admissions Director said, "It wasn't a matter of judgment. There are certain standards at Butler and they have to be met to attend Butler."

In a handwritten letter dated Friday, October 14th, Coach Bill Sylvester said,

"In the rush of events, my real feelings were never put into words with you. Since last August, you have been as much a part of my every day thinking as my own family has been.

Now that the anxiety and frustration has ended from this end, I want to wish you the very best of happiness and success. And as I have always said to you- "things are going to work out well for Garo."

You have a bright future. No one could be more deserving and I am sure that no one will carry success as well as you.

It has been a pleasure in knowing you. You have made many friends and have fans rooting for you from Butler University. You will always be remembered—always welcome.

Sincerely,
Bill Sylvester

You now know the answer to "Who in the hell is that?" Needless to say they didn't "Get that little piss ant outta here."

Garo Yepremian was destined to be welcome in football locker rooms for years to come.

Chapter 8 ✌

After his first experience with football in the NFL with the LIONS against the Baltimore COLTS, Garo's dream of owning a Ford Mustang was not to be deterred. He went to the Ford dealership in Detroit and fell in love with a white Mustang GT 390 with black racing stripes and a black interior. Its four-barrel carburetor, five speeds on the floor and four chrome exhaust pipes made a statement to him. It was a finely tuned marvelous instrument of speed and power. Garo's memories of his old English Ford Anglia faded into the dust of time. He had to have this automobile. The salesman explained that he couldn't sell him the Mustang because it was the only one at the dealership and it was to be used as a demonstration model. Garo asked to see the manager. The manager recognized Garo as the new LIONS kicking phenom. He thought it would be good publicity for the dealership if Garo bought his first car there. He allowed Garo to buy the car for the full sticker price. Garo didn't know that in the United States you could negotiate for lower dollars than the asking price. This was a clean deal-no trade in, no bank loan, write a check for full payment.

After all of the paper work was finished Garo drove north on I-94.

Garo says, "I loved the feel and quickness of the automobile. The new car smell was the nicest perfume I could imagine. This was a luxury automobile masquerading as a sports car. After about an hour I decided to head back to Detroit. It was dark at the interchange and the route markers and direction signs were difficult to see. In the process of trying to find the 'on' ramp to go south I got lost."

That is not too difficult for an experienced driver when trying to read unfamiliar road signs in the dark.

"After some three hours of driving in what I thought was a southerly direction I managed to find my way back to the Leland House hotel. I went to sleep tired and happy."

During the week Garo was able to observe the contact violence of pro football.

"It seemed to me that even in practice the ballplayers were trying to kill each other. I also noted some the young players removing their false teeth before practice."

That week they boarded a plane and headed for San Francisco to play the 49ers. When they got on the bus at the San Francisco airport Coach Gilmer sat in the first seat to the right of the driver, just behind the front door, with his customary chaw of tobacco in his cheek. Garo was in the seat behind Gilmer. They pulled out of the airport. Gilmer squirted a stream of tobacco juice into the front stair well bus. The driver was irritated and told Gilmer to warn him when he was ready to spit and he would stop the bus and open the door. Several times during the long drive from San Francisco airport to the Fairmont Hotel on Nob Hill the bus would stop and Coach Gilmer would spit a stream of tobacco juice through the open door. Ah, the glamour and glory of pro football lives on.

The Fairmont Hotel was the most luxurious place Garo had ever seen.

"I couldn't believe that I was so lucky as to be with an American professional football team."

Later that day, Friday Maclem the equipment man and some other non-playing personnel invited Garo to go on a sightseeing trip with them. They toured Alcatraz and saw the Golden Gate Bridge. Garo was determined to learn as much as he could about the United States. Each time he went to a new city to play he would take in as many sights as possible. The trip to San Francisco was exciting. Quarterback John Brodie was in his tenth season of a fabulous career. Karl Sweetan made his first start at quarterback for the Lions.

On the opening kickoff Kermit Alexander of the 49ers broke out of the pack. Suddenly Garo found out that he was something more than a kicker. He was the only LION between Alexander and the goal. Someone tackled Alexander from behind while Garo was so close to the play that he got caught in the pileup.

Garo said later, "I'm supposed to stay back and watch them and if somebody gets loose I'm supposed to tackle him."

Wayne Walker attempted the first field goal for the LIONS. He missed. In the second quarter Wayne got thrown out of the game by the officials and Alex

Karras had to miss part of the game after taking a hit on the head. Garo kicked a 30-yard field goal in the second quarter-his first successful kick in the NFL. He was still very nervous. He missed three field goals that day. He did manage to make three extra points. Karl Sweetan was having a great day and the Lions were leading 24-20. John Brodie came through in the clutch as he had done so many times before. With three seconds to go he hit Monte Stickles with a 21-yard pass for a touchdown and the win. It was a crowd pleaser for the San Francisco fans. Detroit was now 2-6-0 on the season.

When a team has a losing season underway tension creeps in through every chink in its professional armor. It fills every mental and physical nook and cranny. The players were grumbling about Coach Gilmer's play calling and player substitutions. Gilmer on the other hand was threatening to trade players whom he thought were not giving their best to the team. It was not a happy situation and did nothing to help ease Garo's nervousness.

Vince Lombardi brought the Green Bay PACKERS to Detroit on November 30th. Bart Starr's passing to Elijah Pitts and the running of Jim Taylor riddled the LIONS. The Packers won 31-7. Karl Sweetan connected on a 63-yard pass to Pat Studstill for the lone Detroit touchdown. Wayne Walker kicked the extra point. Garo remembers that he did kickoff in the game. He doesn't remember if it was at the start of the game or the start of the second quarter or the kickoff after the LIONS' only touchdown. What he does remember is that Herb Adderley took the kickoff and came racing downfield. Herb was with the Packers from 1961 to 1969 and finished his career with the Dallas COWBOYS from 1970 to 1972. Herb is now in the pro football HALL OF FAME in Canton, Ohio. On that day in 1966 he was led down the field by the PACKERS six-foot-three-inch two-hundred-and-thirty-five pound linebacker Ray Nitschke. Nitschke is a hall of famer. In Tiger stadium on that Sunday afternoon Nitschke hit Garo across the nose with his forearm. Adderly ran into Nitschke and fumbled the ball. He was able to recover his own fumble while Garo lay bleeding on the ground. The next day the newspaper sports headline read:

LITTLEST LION SHEDS BLOOD IN TIGER STADIUM, SAVES TOUCHDOWN.

Garo said, "That night I held and ice pack to my nose in an attempt to keep the swelling down. I'd wake up in the mornings during the following month with the taste of blood in my mouth. The block by Nitschke was so powerful that I felt lucky to have my teeth still in place."

The grunts, groans, curses, clash of helmets, the thump of pads, sweat, spit and blood in the line "pit" scared the hell out of him. Kicking a football to get an education seemed like a good idea when thought about in far off London. It was a whole new ballgame when experienced closeup. The size of the players was expanded to larger than life by their equipment. Their cat-like quickness in spite of their size added to his fears. It stretches believability to think that a five-foot-seven-inch, 142 pound man could hope to survive long enough to be an important part of such a team effort.

Garo reports, "That injury made me realize that I was playing in a very dangerous game."

He give a lot of credit to Wayne Walker, "Wayne helped me a lot. Even though I threatened to take over the field goal and extra point kicking he continued to help me with little tips about the game and did all he could to boost my confidence."

On November 6th Detroit went to Chicago to play the BEARS. The LIONS played a great defensive game against the BEARS. Wayne Walker kicked a field goal and an extra point and the game was a 10-10 tie. Garo's only field goal attempt was blocked at the 16-yard line.

Coach Gilmer said, "We made a mistake. Instead of the ball being put down six-and-a-half yards behind the line of scrimmage it was placed eight-and-a-half yards back. This gave the outside defensive lineman a straight run at the ball instead of making him circle out of the play."

Garo says, "No matter, I was so nervous that my knees were week and my concentration was non-existent. I could not have completed the attempt under the best of circumstances."

He was definitely in danger of losing his opportunity to play in the NFL. He was in the deep and lonesome valley of depression. He dreaded having to go to Minnesota to play the VIKINGS on the following Sunday.

On Friday, November 11th, Head coach Harry Gilmer called off practice early. The LIONS would play the Minnesota VIKINGS in Bloomington, Minnesota with scrambling Fran Tarkenton at quarterback.

At the end of the practice session assistant coach Karl Taseff gave Garo a royal chewing out. Garo who had shown so much promise in his tryout and was the talk of the town was one for seven in field goal kicking. As a coach Taseff felt that his own job was in jeopardy.

He stuck his nose in Garo's face and yelled in anger and frustration, "This team is paying you big fucking money to kick the fucking football through the fucking goal posts."

He stomped his feet and his face flushed red as he continued, "That fucking soccer style kicking will never go in this league. You're gonna get your fucking ass shipped back home."

Garo hung his head in embarrassment. He had never before been yelled at by a coach. He had missed the thrill of being reamed out by a college or high school football coach. His immediate reaction was fear.

"I thought they were going to send me back to England."

The next day the team flew to Bloomington. The weather was very cold. After checking into the hotel Garo took a walk. He couldn't talk to his teammates. Among them he felt like a stranger in a far and distant land. He was getting a lot of publicity and making many personal appearances. His teammates thought he was a "hotdog," a flash in the pan. As he walked along the street there was ice everywhere. He kicked at small chunks of ice and worried about the condition of the field. He thought about the giant linemen who blocked his kicks and threatened his very existence. It reminded him of David and Goliath in the Old Testament story. David took up the challenge of Goliath in the face of great odds. As a young shepherd boy David practiced with his sling so that he could protect his flock in the wilderness. David had faith in his ability to bring Goliath down with one smooth stone. He carried four extra stones in the event that Goliath's four brothers decided to join the fight. David had faith. Garo knew he had faith and had not been laggard in practice. At that point, he began to talk to Jesus.

He pleaded, "Dear Jesus, please give me the strength and the ability to relax. Don't let them send me back to London."

He felt very close to Jesus that day and he still does.

On Sunday, Coach Gilmer wrote on the blackboard in large block letters KICKERS ON THE FIELD AT 12:45. The place-kickers, Wayne Walker and Garo went on the field as scheduled. Garo was wearing a new set of shoes. When he was working out with the Butler University freshman team Charlie McElfresh, the Butler University equipment man, ordered a new pair of Addias soccer shoes. When the shoes arrived at the University Garo had already been signed by the LIONS. There were no other soccer style kickers on the team. Mr.McElfresh sent the shoes to Garo in Detroit. He was wearing one of the Addias soccer shoes on his left foot and a regular football shoe with longer cleats on his right foot. This mismatched shoe arrangement gave him a familiar soccer shoe on his kicking foot and a good non-slip right leg anchor.

After kicking practice Karl Brettschneider drew Gilmer aside. Brettschneider was the defensive line coach who had extra duty as the place-kicking coach.

"Garo is splitting the middle," Brettschneider told Gilmer in a low voice.

"OK, we'll let Garo do our kicking. Wayne will kickoff and Garo will try our field goals."

Jim Todd the linebacker who had been released to make room for Garo on the LIONS roster was reactivated for this game due to an injury to Bruce McLenna.

The game started and Garo got his first opportunity from 48 yards.

Wayne Rasmussen, the holder looked at Garo and said, "Are you ready?"

Garo says, "I was in a state of panic. My knees were shaking and I felt weak all over. The offensive and defensive men with muscles bulging at the line of scrimmage looked like a human bomb ready to explode. I nodded to Rasmussen and at the same time I felt my face quivering. I raised my right hand to rub my cheek. I saw that the ball was being snapped. I was off stride. The ball hooked off to the right not even close to being a field goal."

Minnesota led 10-0 at the end of the first quarter.

In the second quarter, Garo was sent in to boot a 32-yarder. The VIKINGS called time out to give him a little more time to get nervous. That was a mistake.

"I stood in the LIONS' backfield and looked across the line. I imagined that the opposing linemen were nothing more than a line of ants on the familiar and friendly church wall back in my old home town of Larnaca, Cyprus. That cockroach above the line of ants was in the center of the goal posts. This time when Wayne Rasmussen said, 'Are you ready?' I really was."

The ball was snapped, Garo kicked and it sailed through the uprights.

Garo followed his first field goal with three more

from 26-yards, 15-yards and 20-yards. At half time the LIONS were leading the VIKINGS 12-10. In the third quarter he tried one from 39-yards and missed. A little later he connected from 28-yards for his fifth field goal of the game. Coach Karl Taseff said that he had broken the record for the most field goals in a game. Friday Maclem, the equipment man presented him with the ball. A few minutes later Friday informed him that they had made a mistake he had only tied the record. He took the ball from Garo. In the third quarter Garo had an opportunity to attempt one from the 32-yard line. The kick was good. Garo set a new NFL record for the most field goals in a single game in the forty-seven year history of the NFL. In the fourth quarter he kicked two points after touchdown. His game total was 20 points.

Fran Tarkenton was having a bad day. The VIKINGS got the ball back with 1:04 left in the game. Their offense stalled and they lost the ball on downs.

The final score was Detroit 32-Minnesota-31.

Less than one month after the day he sat in a daze in the locker room in Baltimore wondering how to put his uniform on Garo had broken a record set by Ernie Nevers for the Duluth ESKIMOS in 1926 and tied in 1951 by Bob Waterfield with the Los Angeles RAMS, the Chicago BEARS' Roger LeClerc in 1961 and in 1964 by Jim Bakken with the St. Louis CARDINALS.

Cameras and microphones were everywhere as gregarious Garo talked about his kicking. He did a little adagio dance step to show how he hit the ball with his instep. It was made to order for television. Suddenly he was famous on radio and television and the sports pages of newspapers coast to coast. Garo gives a lot of credit for his success that day to his fellow kicker Wayne Walker who helped him in so many ways during the rough time he was having prior to the Minnesota game.

On the bus going to the airport Wayne laughed and said, "You and me, Garo. We'll negotiate our salaries together next year like Koufax and Drysdale. Maybe we should go for a million between us."

Garo smiled. He finally felt like a contributing member of the team.

While Garo maintained a healthy concern about his kicks his talk with Jesus on that cold and icy Saturday in Minnesota gave him the power to develop a new and lasting feeling of safety and security. Never again would he let fear and anxiety overcome his ability on the playing field. God moves in mysterious ways. The ants and cockroach on the wall in Garo's imagination kept his thoughts calm and gave him a way to avoid his nervous distractions.

On Tuesday following his record breaking performance in Minnesota the DETROIT FREE PRESS and the DETROIT NEWS recorded an event that shows the compassion that Garo has for his fellow human beings. The University of Michigan and the Michigan Kidney Foundation formed the nation's first "walking kidney bank."

Quarterback Karl Sweetan was scheduled to be the first donor in the program. Karl was suffering from injured ribs and Garo volunteered to take Karl's place. The headlines and the pictures in the papers brought much needed attention to this humanitarian project. The headlines read:

FIRST KIDNEY TRANSPLANT BANK FORMED
AT UNIVERSITY HOSPITAL

HERO DEPOSITS AT KIDNEY BANK

Boyce Rensberger, the DETROIT FREE PRESS science writer wrote:

The big toe of the Detroit Lions kicked off the Michigan Kidney Foundation's campaign to make a supply of kidneys available for transplants.

Garo Yepremian, who set a National Football League record Sunday by kicking six field goals to help defeat the Minnesota Vikings, 32-31, signed a pledge card allowing his kidneys to be transplanted at death to a kidney disease victim.

Since the early days of the 20th century when Garo's grandfather worked in Detroit there has been an active Armenian society in that city. The Armenians in Detroit and all across the nation were proud of Garo's success. They had a problem with their identity being confused with Albanians, Ukranians, etc.

Now they could say, "We are of the same national heritage as Garo Yepremian."

The LIONS had to assign two full time secretaries to handle the bags of mail that were beings sent to Garo.

Garo made several appearances at dances and youth functions of St. John's and St. Sarkis Armenian churches in Detroit. He learned not to take a date to those events. As soon as he and his date would be seated at a table people would come over and take him

away to meet their family and friends. It seemed that
all of the Armenian families that had girls of
marriageable age wanted to introduce them to Garo.
Fame demands its due. The girls he dated did not want
to sit at a table alone while Garo made his rounds.

By mid-week attention turned to the following
Sunday's game when the Baltimore COLTS would play
the LIONS in Tiger stadium. Baltimore's Lou Michaels
was the leading field goal kicker in the NFL.
Left-footed, six-foot-two-inch, two-hundred-fifty-pound
Michaels was a veteran of nine seasons in the league
and had made 19 out of 28 field goal attempts and was
25-for-25 on extra points. In contrast Garo would be
playing in his sixth game. The sports writers and
sportscasters had a field day writing and talking about
the forthcoming kicking duel. It was the story of an
upstart young player competing against a veteran star.
The COLTS were predicted to win. The general
consensus was that Garo could not kick as many points
as Johnny Unitas could generate with his arm.

The COLTS were in a tie for the western division
lead with the Green Bay PACKERS. They had plenty
of motivation to win the game. 52,383 eager fans
crowded into TIGER Stadium. After the great
Minnesota win the fans sensed that the team was
playing with new life. They wanted to see the little
kicker in action.

Early in the game the LIONS scored a touchdown
on a running play and Garo kicked the extra point.
At the end of the first quarter the score was 7-0 in
favor of the LIONS. The second quarter was
scoreless. The LIONS went into the clubhouse at
half-time leading 7-0.

In the first few minutes of the 2nd half Detroit intercepted two Unitas passes. Ernie Clark caught a ball that bounced off of John Mackey. Clark's interception led to Garo's first field goal from the 21-yard line. The LIONS extended their lead to 10-0. It is only fair to say that Johnny Unitas was suffering from a sore arm and his passes didn't have their usual snap. The five interceptions made by the LIONS shows that his passes were hanging up by a fraction of a second and the LIONS were taking advantage.

The LIONS were also playing with renewed vigor. Some of the interceptions were very acrobatic in nature. Gary Cuozzo came in to relieve Unitas after the second interception early in the second half. The next Detroit score was a great team effort. Karl Sweetan started on his own 22-yard line. Tom Nowatzke made a big 14-yard run on a draw play up the middle as Sweetan worked the ball to the COLTS 49-yard line. Sweetan threw a long pass to Pat Studstill on the Baltimore 25 who then ran through the defenders and crossed the goal line for a touchdown. After Garo kicked the extra point the LIONS led the COLTS 17-0. The COLTS were anxiously looking at the scoreboard which showed the Green Bay PACKERS leading the Chicago BEARS.

In the fourth quarter Baltimore scored when Cuozzo tossed a short one to tight end John Mackey. Instead of being stopped with a short gain Mackey fought off all of the LIONS tacklers and completed a 64-yard run for the score. Michaels kicked the extra point and the score was now 17-7.

Garo says that run by Mackey was the most

memorable run he ever saw in pro football. It was a bull rush that no one could stop.

The COLTS next took possession after a fumble on the LIONS 16-yard line. Penn State University's great running back Lenny Moore playing in the NFL for the COLTS angled in from the 7-yard line for the score. Another Lou Michaels extra point and the score was 17-14 with 9-minutes left in the game.

The COLTS kicked off. The LIONS took the ball deep into COLT territory. Garo came on to kick a 17-yard field goal. The LIONS defensive team dug in and held off the COLTS and the game ended with a Detroit victory 20-14. It was a stunning upset and sweet revenge for the 45-14 walloping Baltimore gave Detroit in Garo's first game.

The LIONS vaulted out of last place over Minnesota and Chicago and into fifth place. Their record was 4-6-1.

Four days after the Baltimore game the San Francisco 49ers came into Detroit for the Thanksgiving Day game. The LIONS' fans draped home made signs around the stadium which said "Karl to Pat," some signs said "Garo Go."

It was not to be in this game. John Brodie was in top form. The final score was San Francisco 41–Detroit 14. Garo had no opportunity to kick a field goal.

In the post game interview, Detroit guard John Gordy said, "We were flatter than hell. We didn't hit anybody all afternoon. It just got away from us and they laid it on."

On Sunday, December 4th, the LIONS flew to Los Angeles to play the RAMS in Memorial Coliseum.

Garo played tourist and did some sightseeing around the famed movie capital. He followed his plan to learn as much as possible about his adopted country.

The RAMS kept the game well in hand. Their defensive unit with Merlin Olsen in the line kept the LIONS at bay. The only LIONS score was a field goal that Garo kicked from the 23-yard line. The final score-Los Angeles 23-Detroit 3.The final game of the 1966 season was scheduled for December 11th when Minnesota would visit Tiger Stadium. Garo and Krikor were happily awaiting a visit from their parents. Garo sent his parents money for the trip and rented a house for a month to accommodate his parents on their first visit to the United States. The house was warm even though there was lots of snow on the ground. Actually it was a much nicer home than the one they were living in London.

When Azadouhi and Sarkis sat in the stands to watch this game that their son was playing they were mystified by the strange antics on the field.

The team went into the huddle. Azadouhi turned to a fan seated next to her and asked, "Are they praying?"

The fan was drinking and was in a very talkative mood. Every time a play was executed he would explain what was happening.

Under her breath Azadouhi prayed for Garo, "Please God help him-whatever he is doing."

At halftime the TV people took them on the field for an interview.

Azadouhi said, "We are trying to like it. We learn little by little. At first we thought they were trying to kill each other."

The VIKINGS didn't kill the LIONS but they did

get revenge for the earlier game they lost to the LIONS. Fran Tarkenton riddled the LIONS with passes and the defensive unit held them to three field goals and one touchdown. Garo connected from the 43-yard line and followed that with one from the 29. Later he finished with a short kick from the 17-yard line. With one extra point and three field goals Garo added 10 points to his total.

At the end of the game Coach Harry Gilmer, with a fresh chew of tobacco in his jaw, put his arm around Garo and said, "Garo, you are my man."

Garo ended the season with 13 field goals and 11 point-after-touchdown kicks. His 50 points made him the highest scorer on the team. The LIONS finished the season with 4 wins-9 losses-and 1 tie.

One highlight of the LIONS season was Pat Studstill's sixty-seven pass catches for 1,266 yards for tops in the league.

Green Bay won the Western Division title 12-2-0 and Dallas took the Eastern Conference with 10-3-1.

In the NFL Championship game Green Bay defeated Dallas 34-27.

The Super Bowl was played at Memorial Coliseum in Los Angeles and the Green Bay PACKERS defeated the Kansas City CHIEFS 35-10.

Those were the glory years for Vince Lombardi and Green Bay.

Chapter 9 ❧

The Yepremians spent Christmas in Detroit. Krikor, his wife Markanna and son Sarko, Sarkis and Azadouhi, eleven-year-old brother Berj and Garo went to a Christmas party at St. John's Armenian church. Garo felt that he was in touch with his roots in Detroit. At St. John's he met an old man who had roomed with his grandfather during that cold winter when they had to burn some of the furniture to keep warm. Sarkis and Garo were eager to hear about old Krikor. The old man was able to give them good information about Krikor's life in the United State. Sarkis then related the sad tale about how his father was murdered and the chain of events that had brought them to Detroit. The interlaced patterns of fate are difficult to explain. For Garo the answer lies in his simple faith in a higher power that guides his life. So many times during personal adversity he has been able reach out and gather strength through prayer.

The off season was a busy time for Garo. He took a job at Charlie's Ford Agency on Jefferson Street in Detroit. His name and fame in the Detroit papers gave him an opportunity to do valuable public relations work. Garo was in the mood for a new automobile. He began to find fault with the Mustang he had bought early in his first season. He thought the rear end was too light for the driving he liked to do. He fell in love with a 1967 Thunderbird. It was silver gray with a black landau roof and a black interior and suicide doors. The car came with the new owner's name inscribed on a plaque placed on the dashboard. It was a sporty car for a man of sports.

There were two memorable speaking engagements during that first off season. He flew to New York where Father Mampre Kouzouian picked him up and took him to Union City, New Jersey. This was the same Father Mampre who told young Garo that his robes were not too hot because they had fans built into them. In Union City, at the Holy Cross Armenian Church Men's Club Sports Night he shared the speaker's podium with Allie Sherman, who had just completed his sixth year as head coach of the New York GIANTS. Father Mampre was the pastor of a church in Hackensack, New Jersey. Garo served as a sub-deacon at the altar at the Sunday service. He spent a couple of days in New York City where he visited the Empire State building and walked around Manhattan looking at the tall buildings.

Art Arkelian, an Armenian who owns radio and TV stations, invited Garo to the WWYN sports banquet in Erie, Pennsylvania. Garo shared the spotlight with Brooks Robinson, the Baltimore Orioles Golden

Glove 3rd baseman, Tommy Helms, of the Cincinnati Reds who was named baseball's 1966 rookie of the year and Herb Score whose fast ball had been timed at more than 100-miles-per-hour.

Jack Polancy, writing in the Inside Sports column in Erie said, "and this time it was also apparent that we had met the nicest person in professional football."

Garo was a polite 22-year-old man who had the knack of turning tales about football into funny events even when in truth they had been extremely stressful situations.

Garo was hired to be an extra in the movie "The Paper Lion."

George Plimpton was a successful writer who told of his experiences in unusual situations. George would train for and participate in the events he was writing about. His PAPER LION movie was being shot at St. Andrews School in Boca Raton, Florida. When Garo and his brother Krikor drove down the Sunshine Parkway they were pleasantly surprised by the beautiful weather. It reminded them of the weather on the island of Cyprus.

Alan Alda and super model Loreen Hutton starred in the movie. Garo was getting a lot of publicity because of his record breaking kicking performance against the Minnesota VIKINGS and it was a natural selection to have him in a movie about an ordinary man playing with a professional team. He filled in on some of the back ground scenes and was shown attending team meetings. He enjoyed amusing the cast and crew with his warmup exercises. He bounced the ball from knee to knee, to the top of his head, from toe to toe all the while showing wonderful control of the ball. Alan Alda loved to watch Garo's exhibitions. It was an example of body control not unlike that which an actor wants to achieve. He gave Garo a white shirt with a blue "0" number that he wore in the film. Garo kept it as a treasured memento of his movie making days.

Krikor went along for a short vacation while Garo was making the movie. He left Florida and went home to Detroit before the movie was finished.

The day the movie shooting ended Garo got a phone call from Krikor.

Krikor said, "I need you here by tomorrow. The sooner you get here the better. I need a baby sitter for Sarko."

Markanna, his wife had left home for a permanent separation.

Garo left Boca Raton and started the long drive to Detroit. On Florida's Sunshine Parkway the water pump on his Thunderbird went out and he had to get towed to a garage for repairs. After the water pump was replaced he drove on to Atlanta where he spent the night. Early in the morning he noticed that the weather was getting colder. As he made his way toward Ohio the overcast became heavy and the clouds looked ominous. In Ohio, he ran into a big snowstorm and there was only one traffic lane open. Visibility was terrible. He knew he had to find a place to stay for the night. His eyes were tired and he was fighting sleep.

He drove slowly along and began looking for a motel. NO VACANCY signs were on at all of the motels. Finally, in Lima, Ohio, he saw a dim neon sign that said JESUS SAVES MISSION–WELCOME two doors down the street another flashing red neon sign said LIQUOR-SALOON-ROOMS. He decided to give it a try.

He got out of the car wearing his navy blue cashmere coat. He was definitely overdressed for that part of town. When he walked into the saloon he thought the men there looked like a group of thugs especially when one of the men at the bar lifted a foaming glass of beer, took a swig and said, "Hey, look at the dude in the fancy coat."

Remember, Garo was not familiar with "blue collar" America. He had been in the country less than a year and most of his time had been spent with the LIONS or with people connected to big time sports.

When he asked the bartender for a room the bartender yelled, "Yo! Mabel, this guy needs a room."

Mabel was wiping a table and carrying on a loud conversation with the customers. Mabel might have been considered pretty if, as the line in the country song goes "I like my women a little on the trashy side." She looked wise in the ways of the world far beyond her years.

She came over and said, "Mister, we do have a room upstairs. You better look at it first. That damn room's as cold as ice."

Garo followed her up three flights of steps. They walked down a narrow hallway. Many of the room doors were open. Garo saw men lying on the beds smoking cigarettes.

Most of them would yell "Hi, Mabel" as they passed by.

Garo says, "By this time I was looking for any kind of excuse to get out of the place. I thought I might be in another spot similar to the pleasure dens of Beirut."

Mabel showed him the room. The light from the neon sign on the front of the building was casting an eerie, blinking, red glow on the walls.

Garo said, "It is very cold. I don't think I will take it."

They went back downstairs and Garo walked through the bar expecting to be tackled at any moment.

Garo, "When I got to my car I felt like I had escaped with my life."

It is only fair to say that in later years he realized that he probably had stopped at a place where over-the-road truck drivers stayed. Sleeper cabs were not as popular in those days. The mode of dress and the natural camaraderie of the trucking crowd were unfamiliar to Garo. He felt threatened by their strange ways.

Garo says, "I jumped into my Thunderbird and decided to fight sleep and go on to Detroit. I got there in the wee hours of the morning and collapsed on the bed. I woke up late in the day and called Krikor."

Krikor said, "Where have you been. I've been worried."

Krikor explained that he had called Mom in London and that she would be there in a few days. Garo baby sat with Sarko until Mom and brother Berj arrived. Berj was enrolled in a Catholic school. Sarkis joined Azadouhi in the States about seven weeks later. A short time after that they decided to buy a house at 11-mile road and Lahser Road in Southfield, Michigan. Garo had trouble getting a mortgage because he had not established a credit rating. He thought that because he didn't owe any money he would be a good prospect for a mortgage. He found out that it didn't work that way. Having established credit was important in the American way of life. After a time with some help and advice from some Armenian friends who owned a dry cleaning establishment they were able to buy the house.

Garo's roots were plunging deeper into American soil.

Chapter 10 🍂

The LIONS training camp was scheduled to open at Cranbrook High School on July 7th. Garo's friends told him that Cranbrook was really a nice place. It had a multi-level swimming pool and they described the place in terms that made it sound like Club Med.

When the players reported to training camp they were told to get a physical and take their shots and come back to camp in the afternoon. At Cranbrook they were housed in tiny rooms with no air conditioning. The practice field was about 500 yards down the hill from the training room. In the afternoon the players were made to run laps and take endless calisthenics. With grass drills and up and downs Club Med it was not.

Three days after training camp started Krikor came to see him.

Krikor asked, "How do you feel?

Garo groaned, "I hurt in every part of my body."

He had never been subjected to such rigorous

exercise. During the off season the LIONS bought out the remaining time on Harry Gilmer's contract. Management was convinced that the team would never give Gilmer one hundred percent effort. They hired ex-LIONS linebacker Joe Schmidt as head coach. In an attempt to rejuvenate the LIONS William Clay Ford brought in several rookies.

There was Nick Eddy, from Notre Dame, Mel Farr from UCLA, Lem Barney from Jackson State and Paul Naumoff from the University of Tennessee. There were a total of twenty five free agents in camp. Joe Schmidt played from 1953 to 1965 and was from the old school and thought that a kicker should also play a regular position on the team. Garo felt like an outsider. The players did nothing to make him feel like a part of the team. He really wanted to get in there and scrimmage with the them.

He lamented, "I watch them and I know they are killing themselves out there. It would be nice to get out there with them, but I know I would get killed. If I play, I will get hurt. If I get hurt I cannot kick and then where am I?"

He knew that if he got hurt he would have no chance at all of making the team. In return the other players thought he was cocky. He wore a beret to protect his balding head from the hot July sun. To cover up his inner feelings of insecurity he talked to the sports reporters in an extremely positive manner. He was good "copy" for them. He talked about being a better kicker than he was in the previous season. He wanted to shoot for a seventy-five-percent kicking average. He said that he should reach a point where he would never miss a kick that was less than 50-yards long. Those were pretty strong words for someone who was fairly new in the NFL. The coaches and the players resented the thought that anyone could be that much of a specialist in their sport. They thought a kicker should have the big bruises and sore muscles common to the game.

In 1967 the NFL was reorganized into two conferences as follows:

EASTERN CONFERENCE

CAPITOL DIVISION	*CENTURY DIVISION*
Dallas COWBOYS	Cleveland BROWNS
Philadelphia EAGLES	New York GIANTS
Washington REDSKINS	St.Louis CARDINALS
New Orleans SAINTS	Pittsburgh STEELERS

WESTERN CONFERENCE

COASTAL DIVISION	*CENTRAL DIVISION*
Los Angeles RAMS	Green Bay PACKERS
Baltimore COLTS	Chicago BEARS
San Francisco 49ers	Detroit LIONS
Atlanta FALCONS	Minnesota VIKINGS

1967 marked the first time that an American Football League team beat a National Football League team.

The Denver BRONCOS defeated Detroit 13-7 in a pre-season game on August 5th.

The 48th NFL season opened on Sunday, September 15th. Record crowds totaling 464,007 fans saw the opening games. Detroit played at Green Bay and Green Bay was picked to win. The LIONS with Milt Plum at quarterback had a good day. They came away with a 17-17 tie.

The LIONS had intercepted four Bart Starr passes and Alex Karras had a good day on the Detroit defensive line. Vince Lombardi didn't like the results at all. His Packers were trying to win their third championship in a row. Garo did not play in that game.

The LIONS followed up with a victory over the BROWNS in Detroit. Milt Plum had a good day in the passing department and rookie Mel Farr ran like the wind. Garo scored a 33-yard field goal and kicked four extra points. The final score was 31-14 favor of Detroit. Lou "The Toe" Groza kicked two extra points for the BROWNS.

The LIONS suffered three losses in a row after the BROWNS game. On October 22nd Karl Sweetan started his first game of the season and the LIONS beat Atlanta 24-3. Wayne Walker did the kicking. Detroit won its second game in a row on October 29th beating San Francisco 45-3. Karl Sweetan was the quarterback and Garo kicked a 26-yard field goal in the 3rd quarter to go along with his six extra point kicks.

Karl Sweetan left Wake Forest in his senior year to play in the Canadian Football League. He was then drafted by the LIONS and played for the Pontiac

ARROWS before coming to the LIONS. Karl tried to emulate some of the famed hard drinking quarterbacks of old. Once before a game he picked Garo up at home. He stopped and bought a six pack of beer and consumed it on the way to the stadium. Illegal drugs were not a problem in those days, however some of the players did manage to abuse alcohol.

By the beginning of November, 1967, there was unrest among the players.

Creighton Miller attorney for the NFL Players Association said, "A labor union in pro football may seriously and adversely change the game."

He went on to say, "A union would hurt the game's public image."

Overall Detroit had a lackluster season. On November 12th they managed to tie the VIKINGS while fumbling the ball eleven times setting a new record for the most fumbles in a game. Garo did not play in that game.

The LIONS finished the season with five wins-seven losses and two ties. Mel Farr was named the rookie of the year and the LIONS Lem Barney was the defensive rookie of the year. Garo sensed that head coach Joe Schmidt wanted to get rid of him and that the fans were beginning to forget about him.

During the off season in the winter of 1968 Garo took a two week vacation to London to see his many friends there.

Garo says, "I learned that the old adage that says 'you can't go home again' is true. My friends had changed. I had changed and our common interests were not the same anymore. I was homesick for the United States before the end of my vacation."

He spent a lot of time in his newly rented apartment that winter watching television. He became an avid fan of the Andy Griffith show. Andy, Barney Fife and Goober helped him shed the tensions generated by life in the fast football world.

In the summer of 1968 Garo reported to camp at Cranbrook High and thought he had a pretty good training camp and exhibition season. The LIONS had drafted Jerry DePoyster from Wyoming. DePoyster came with the reputation of being an all around kicker. He had kicked a lot of long field goals in college. He could punt, kickoff and kick field goals.

During training camp Garo was kicking better than DePoyster. However, the players were rooting for Jerry.

Garo. "On the day of the final cut Joe Schmidt called me into his office and said that soccer style kicking would never go in the NFL and that straight on kicking would always be around. He offered to put me on the taxi squad and would pay me three-hundred-dollars per week. I refused to take the deal and walked away."

That evening as Garo was discussing the situation with Krikor and his Mom and Dad the phone rang. It was Russ Thomas of the LIONS.

Russ said, "Garo, why don't you come back tomorrow morning."

Garo said he would come in. The next day when he went to Russ Thomas' office Joe Schmidt was there.

Russ said, "Look we're putting you on the taxi squad to give you more experience. In order to do that we'll let you play with the Michigan ARROWS in the Continental League."

Garo said, "I can't afford to play for three-hundred-dollars a week. Give me my full salary and I will go on the taxi squad."

Russ said, "OK, we'll also give you one-hundred-dollars per game when you play with the ARROWS."

What an unusual situation. Garo was demoted and making more money at the same time. He played in the Continental League and made seven out of ten field goals. One was a 48-yarder. The LIONS were having problems kicking field goals and Garo thought that they might call him up. It didn't happen. The LIONS went through the season without him.

Russ Thomas said, "You'll have a better opportunity next year. We feel that you will be ready."

During the off season Garo was classified 1-A in the draft. He now had his green card and was eligible to be drafted. People in the LIONS public relations department advised him to go to England and declare that he only came to the United States to work and therefore would not have to go in the United States Army.

Garo said, "Look, this is going to be my home. I'll do whatever is necessary to be a good citizen."

The LIONS Vice President, Edward J. Anderson said, "You don't have to be a full time soldier. Go into the Army Reserve where you serve six months active duty and go in the reserves for five-and-a-half years."

Garo joined the Army and took basic training at Ft. Leonard Wood, Missouri. He spent eight weeks in basic training where at the age of twenty-five he was the oldest person in the unit. He looked older because of his balding head. Most of the younger boys got homesick. The Sergeant pushed Garo hard. He wanted to see what he could do. He became squad leader. Garo lost ten pounds during basic and weighed in at one-hundred-and-sixty pounds. Garo says it helped him physically and mentally to know that he could walk eight miles to the rifle range. His confidence rose dramatically. After eight weeks of basic training he was classified as a cook and sent to Ft. Carson, Colorado, near Colorado Springs. When Garo's group got there the regular cooks were busy feeding a group of veterans returning from Vietnam. Garo went into the mess hall and made eggs for the other men in his group.

The Mess Sergeant saw him and said, "You stay here."

Garo was kept at work in that mess hall. It was a good unit. They fed the vets well as they came to Ft. Carson to be reclassified. While Garo was there he got a letter from Russ Thomas who advised him to stay in shape. He also sent Garo six footballs for practice purposes. The air in Colorado was thin and Garo reported back to Russ by letter that he was kicking the football farther than ever.

Garo got out of the Army in September and reported to the LIONS. He was told that he would be released. The LIONS had signed Errol Mann to kick field goals while Jerry DePoyster would do the punting.

The LIONS had to keep Garo for four games because of the NFL rule regarding players returning from military service. This gave Garo another year of eligibility in the league's pension plan. Garo practiced with the team but did not go to any games. The other players didn't know that he was to be released. One day when Garo was walking down the hall a player banged into him on purpose and called him a foreigner.

Garo showed a rare touch of anger as he yelled, "You are a draft dodger. I served in the Army. I would have gone into combat or done anything the army asked me to do. I'm more of an American than you are."

The player had been classified 4-f because he claimed he had a lower back problem. The final four weeks with the LIONS were not easy ones. Garo is in the ranks of the unemployed. His financial situation is precarious at best.

Where could he go? Where could he look for help? It is a time for a close look at the priorities in his life.

PART 2 &

PART 2

Chapter 11 ❧

Garo continued in the dismal ranks of the unemployed. No other team called for his services. To add to his humiliation his friends became cold and scarce.

Garo searched for work. He thought he might be able to get a job as a soccer coach. His limited schooling and lack of a degree in education prevented that hope. He couldn't find a job. He applied for work on the Ford Motor Company assembly line. They didn't need him. He felt like an unloved stray dog with fleas.

Each evening when brother Berj came home from school he and Garo would play ping pong in the basement. Garo became a very good ping pong player. He didn't go out very much because he felt unimportant. He had lost his identity.

In his prayers he asked, "Lord, what have I done. Why am I forsaken."

It was not a good time for the Yepremians. Krikor was going through a devastating divorce. He was the only one in the family earning money. Krikor knew that they weren't making enough money to live on. Azadouhi decided to use her seamstress skills and began to take in sewing jobs. That turned out to be a lot of work with very little return.

One evening Krikor came home and asked, "Mom, can you make neckties."

She said, "Yes, if you give me one to take apart I'll get the pattern."

She made a bunch of wild ties. Krikor took them to work and sold them. An item appeared in a newspaper that said "Garo the tiebreaker is now a tiemaker." A lot of little boutiques and stores wanted to buy the ties.

About that time Garo got a letter from the Internal Revenue Service stating that he was going to be audited. There was a two-hundred-fifty-dollar discrepancy in his tax return. Garo went to the LIONS office which was about a block away from TIGER Stadium and saw Vice President Edward J. Anderson. Mr. Anderson was well respected by the players. He was courteous and always neatly dressed in the latest fashion. His demeanor and office surroundings indicated that he was a neat and orderly man. Mr. Anderson said he was familiar with the IRS problem and would take care of it.

In the course of the conversation while he was typing the letter for Garo to send to the IRS he asked, "What are you doing?"

Garo said, "I can't find a job."

Mr. Anderson said, "Garo you are too good a kicker not to be playing for a team in the NFL. You should be calling teams to apply for a position."

Garo explained, "I don't have money to pay for telephone calls.

Mr. Anderson said, "Do you mind if I write some letters for you?"

Garo replied, "I am happy to accept the offer. I suggest that you write to San Francisco, Green Bay, San Diego and Miami. I know those teams could use a good kicker."

Garo has always thought that for everything bad that happened to him something good was returned to him.

Don Shula played professional football with the Cleveland BROWNS and the Baltimore COLTS. He had been a defensive aid with the Detroit LIONS. He replaced Weeb Ewbank as coach of the Baltimore Colts and held that position through 1969.

Don moved from his coaching position in Baltimore to become the head coach of the Miami DOLPHINS in 1970. When he got the letter from Edward J. Anderson he called Garo and said he would give him a tryout. He offered a contract for the NFL minimum of $13,000 per year. He asked Garo to report to training camp in Miami in July.

Garo flew to Miami and called to have someone pick him up at the airport. They said they couldn't come because the players were on strike. Charlie Calahan, the Miami Public Relations director told Garo to go to the Howard Johnson motel across the street from Miami University because the veteran players were practicing there. Garo went to the motel and moved in.

He didn't have much cash and he didn't have a credit card. He called Krikor and explained the situation. Every couple of days he would hitchhike over to Coral Gables and pick up money that Krikor would wire to him.

Garo read the news reports about how the long smoldering differences between the National Football League Players Association and the owners group caused Commissioner Pete Rozelle to order the start of training camps to be moved to the following Tuesday. NFLPA President John Mackey, tight end of the Baltimore Colts, sent letters ordering the veteran players not to report to training camp. Garo knew that there were strong feelings attached to the football negotiations. The owners called it a strike and the players called it a lockout.

The College All Stars went out on a one-day stoppage of practice to show support of the professional players. The Tribune Charities game scheduled to be played on July 31st between the All Stars and the Kansas City Chiefs was in jeopardy. The sides in the dispute were deadlocked on July 21st. On July 22nd the owners agreed to accept a meeting with the Federal Mediation and Conciliation Service.

Tough old George Halas, the pioneer owner of the Chicago Bears said, "Mediation is foreign to football and so are terms like union, strike and lockout."

During the course of the meetings the Players Association agreed to let the Kansas City Chiefs report to camp for the All Star game. On Tuesday, July 28th Garo was disappointed to hear that the owners had broken off the talks. On Wednesday, July 29th, the owners opened the camps to any veteran player who wanted to come in. Only a few reported and they felt that they had special reasons to try to get in shape. The 37th All Star game was played in front of 69,940 fans in Chicago. Thirty-five-year-old quarterback Len Dawson of the Chiefs showed his mastery of the game as the Chiefs defeated the All Stars 24-3. The Chiefs had only five days of practice.

Karl Taseff the former LIONS coach who berated Garo prior to his record breaking performance in Minnesota moved to the DOLPHINS to be an assistant coach to his former team mate Don Shula. Karl called Garo every day to try to get him to come in and be a "scab." Garo wouldn't do it. He stuck to his guns. Nick Bouniconti, the player representative called Krikor and told him that Garo was damned if he became a "scab."

He said, "Garo's chances of getting the job are slim and even if he does get the job no one will protect him when he kicks."

The threat of crippling injuries is no joke in the NFL. Nick advised Garo to stay out of camp until the strike ended.

On Monday, August 3rd, the football labor wars were over and the players headed for camp. A heavy schedule of exhibition games would begin on the following weekend. The opening day of the season would be on September 20th. Garo reported to camp.

Nick Bouniconti asked, "Why have you come to the Miami DOLPHINS. We have Karl Kremser from the University of Tennessee. Karl is a soccer style kicker who had a good year in 1969."

Garo replied, "This is the only team that would give me a chance."

In Camp at Biscayne College Don Shula called the team together.

Garo listened carefully as Shula said, "We've lost some valuable time because of the strike. I'm going to ask you to work very hard. Instead of two-a-day we will have four-a-day workouts."

He gave them a schedule that started at 7:30am. After an hour they would take a break and come back at 9:30 and work until noon. After a noon break they would return at 2:00pm to review their morning's work. Their third workout would be finished by 5:00pm. Dinner would be at 6:00 and then back on the field at 7:30pm for a walk through and then into the meeting room until the 11:00pm curfew.

Shula said, "Seeing that today is our first day together we'll start our program with strength and durability tests."

He went on to say that everyone would be timed in the 40-yard dash and the 12-minute run. Garo didn't understand what the 12-minute run meant.

He thought, "I guess I'll find out."

The players were put in groups with quarterbacks and kickers together, wide receivers and defensive backs next in another group, linebackers had their own group and all offensive and defensive linemen were in a group. Shula ordered then to start running.

He said, "You have to run for 12-minutes and do at least six laps around the field."

The July sun was hot and there was high humidity. Physically, Garo was unprepared to run. He was under the impression that all he had to do was kick. At the end of one lap he thought he was going to die. At the end of three laps his legs just wouldn't go anymore. That's when he started walking. The coaches encouraged him to run. Karl Kremser was his main competition for the kicking job. Karl ran his six laps easily. Jimmy Keyes, the other kicker candidate was a linebacker out of Kentucky University. He had no trouble running his laps.

At the first night meeting Shula said he had some rules that had to be followed. Anyone late for a team meeting would be fined $25.00 and $25.00 per minute for each additional minute of lateness. Each player would be assigned a weight limit. The fine for being overweight was $25.00 plus $25.00 per pound per day as long as the player was overweight. Shula went on to say that if a player missed a flight to a game he would be fined $500.00 and would have to arrange for a flight at his own expense. Furthermore, he expected a 100% effort from everyone.

Room assignments were handed out. Karl Kremser and Garo were housed in the same room in the dormitory. Garo was dead tired after his first day in the DOLPHINS camp. However, unlike his experience in Detroit, he felt that he was a full fledged member of the training camp team.

Each day at kicking practice Garo would try to outdo Karl. If Karl kicked from 40-yards Garo would move to the 47-yard line. Many DOLPHIN fans were in the stands to see the team practice. The fans would cheer each time Garo made a long one.

After a while Karl said, "This is turning into a circus."

He then left. Garo began kicking from the 57-yard line and had the crowd all worked up. They yelled and applauded. Don Shula looked across from the other practice field and noticed that the fans were responding to Garo's performance. That evening Garo's leg muscles were aching.

"Oh God, I'll never make this team," he thought.

The left side of his groin, his left knee and his right hamstring were hurting badly. He didn't want anyone to know that he was suffering. He rubbed himself with liniment and tried to get some sleep. When Karl Kremser came into the room he got angry about the smell and sprayed cologne around in an attempt to cover the smell of liniment.

Sometime during that first week, Nick Bouniconti called Garo to his room and said, "Garo, you're kicking the ball pretty good but you're wasting your time here. Kremser is a good kicker and he had a great season last year."

Garo replied, "Nick, beggars can't be choosers. No other team gave me a chance. I will do the best I can. If I do well in the exhibition season some other team might pick me up."

Within a couple of weeks Garo was given a new room assignment. His roommate was Doug Swift, a linebacker from Amherst. Doug hadn't been drafted by any NFL team and had been cut by a team in the Canadian Football League. Garo and Doug were the freest of free agents. The other players called them the odd couple.

Doug was a messy devil may care kind of man and Garo was meticulous in his habits. Doug liked health foods. He was somewhat of a fanatic about it. He and Garo went to the fruit market and bought a bushel of oranges and a crate of carrots. Doug had a juicer and made orange and carrot drinks which he said were good for him. Most of the players would try anything that might give them an edge in performance. Doug did well in practice and his teammates begged him to give them some of his health juice. There was a minor problem. The pulp and orange peels that were tossed into the wastebasket became the breeding ground for fruit flies. By the end of the week Garo was fighting hard to get rid of the plague of fruit flies.

Doug was fun loving and had an upbeat personality. He owned a Dodge convertible that provided wonderful transportation. On the players day off, Doug, Garo and others would drive over to Miami Beach. Sometimes they would go into a bar and order beers. While he was not a drinker Garo would order a beer and take small sips so he could be a part of the group.

The camaraderie with his friends and Don Shula's rules, regulations and overall command of the team made him feel like part of a winning organization. In contrast to Detroit where there was an offensive unit and a defensive unit which caused the other players to feel left out Don Shula stressed that there was an offensive unit, a defensive unit and special teams. He knew that a winning football team had to get peak performance out of every man on the roster. His discipline and team management made everyone feel that he was part of the winning combination.

In any world class event it only takes a small failure to separate the winners from the losers. A super bowl quality football team is like a smooth running machine. Every nut, bolt, cog and wheel must do its job. An Indianapolis 500 mile race is lost if someone in the pits fails to carry out his duties to perfection. A few seconds translates into a long distance at 200 miles-per-hour. And so it is with football, a yard here and a yard there, made or lost, can mean the difference between victory and defeat. Make no mistake about it, the players in the NFL are the cream of the crop. The difference between winners and loser is very narrow indeed.

In the exhibition season the DOLPHINS beat the Pittsburgh STEELERS 16-10, the Cincinnati BENGALS 20-10 and the San Francisco 49ers 17-7. It was the first time in the DOLPHINS history that they won three in a row. On the following Sunday they defeated the Baltimore COLTS in front of a record 76,712 fans in the Orange Bowl.

The National Football League lost a great name when Vince Lombardi died on September 3rd, 1970. The legendary coach was eulogized for his spectacular career as a coach for the Green Bay PACKERS and as an outstanding motivator of team play. His name and deeds will live forever in the chronicles of football history.

Garo worked hard and was in good physical condition. In the exhibition games he was four-for-four in field goal attempts and his kickoffs were going deep. Nevertheless, Don Shula called him to the office at the time of the final 1970 roster cut.

He said, "I'm going with Karl Kremser. He's the incumbent and doing well. I'll put you on the taxi squad."

Joe Thomas, the General Manager said, "We'll pay you $300.00 per week."

Garo replied, "Mr. Thomas can't you make it $350.00 so I can live like a decent human being."

Joe said, "You're lucky to get the $300.00 because our team owner Joe Robbie doesn't want to keep the Armenian guy around since we don't need him."

Garo shut his mouth and took the job.

The first regular game of the 1970 season pitted the DOLPHINS against the Boston PATRIOTS. With Quarterback Bob Griese and receiver Paul Warfield working to perfection in the passing game the DOLPHINS were heavily favored to win. Garo sat in the stands to watch the game. As a taxi squad player he practiced with the team and traveled with them. However, he could not dress for a game unless another player was deactivated to make room for him on the roster.

In the first game Karl Kremser was sent in to kick a field goal from the 21-yard line. He missed. The whole team was flat and the DOLPHINS lost 27-14. Doug Swift had made the team and was one of the starting linebackers. To celebrate his good fortune he and Garo started looking for an apartment. They saw an ad in the papers for an apartment in Miami Beach. When they got there they realized that the rent would be more than they could afford to pay. Doug was making $14,000. per year and Garo was earning the minimum $13,000. per year. The apartment manager was flattered because two Miami Dolphins wanted to rent an apartment in his complex.

He said, "We'll make a special deal at a lower price if you want to move in here. But first let me show you around."

Garo and Doug were well received by the other tenants they met.

The apartments were very nice and the manager kept saying, "I know the rent is high. But, look at the view."

After the tour the manager said, "These apartments normally rent for $2500. per month. For you, we'll reduce it to $1500. per month."

The boys said goodbye as graciously as possible.

As they were going down in the elevator Garo said, "We are crazy to think that we could afford to live here."

Doug replied, "Yes, but look at the view."

They finally located a place that they could afford. An apartment near Miami Springs. Doug thought that Garo would be activated. Garo felt confident because he was doing well in practice.

On Saturday, September 27th, the team flew to Houston to play the OILERS in the Astrodome. Shula's procedure was to take the team to the field the night before a game and practice for the action on the following day. Karl Kremser was under pressure. In practice he missed kicks from the 30-yard line. Garo and Karl took turns kicking. Garo did well and Karl performed poorly.

Shula said, "Practice is over."

Karl said, "I want to do some more kickoffs."

Garo said the same. Shula watched from the sideline. Some of the traveling Miami press people were in the stands and sensed that something was in the air.

Shula called Karl and Garo over and said, "Karl, I'm putting you on the two week move list. Garo will kick tomorrow."

Garo was excited although he felt sorry for Karl who stood there with tears in his eyes.

He told Doug quietly, "I'm kicking tomorrow."

Bob Sheridan, an announcer for WGBS in Miami, sensed that something had happened. He came over and spoke to Garo who told him that he would kick in tomorrow's game. Bob liked Garo and hoped that he would make the team.

Garo said, "I have two weeks to do well or Karl will come back."

That night he called Detroit and asked his Mom and Krikor to pray for him.

The next day in the Astrodome Garo kicked a 40-yard field goal and another from the 31-yard line. The DOLPHINS won the game 20-14. It was a wonderful flight back to Miami.

The following week the DOLPHINS were to play the Oakland RAIDERS in a Saturday night game in the Orange Bowl. The DOLPHINS had never beaten the RAIDERS and this was the first regular season game at home under Don Shula's coaching. At game time torrential rains were falling and the winds were whipping around in the stadium. The artificial turf was under several of inches of water. When Garo saw the weather conditions and all of that water on the field he thought his chances of kicking a field goal were slim indeed. The players sloshed around and finished the first quarter with no score.

On the first play of the second quarter Miami rookie Curtis Johnson intercepted a Daryle Lamonica pass. Quarterback Bob Griese and the Miami DOLPHINS offensive team took the field. When they broke out of the huddle, Griese rifled a pass to Paul Warfield and the former Ohio State star ran all the way for a 49-yard touchdown. Garo came in an kicked the extra point and the score was 7-0 favor the DOLPHINS.

The Oakland RAIDERS moved the ball well but the DOLPHINS defensive unit held its ground and George Blanda came in an kicked a field goal from the 12-yard line making the score 7-3 Miami.

With very little time left in the first half the DOLPHINS had the ball in RAIDER territory on fourth down. Don Shula called for the punting team.

Garo yelled at Coach Shula and said, "Coach! I can make that field goal."

It looked like an impossible shot. The wind was driving the rain straight into the faces of the offensive team. It would be a 47-yard kick.

Shula again commanded, "Punting team."

Garo pleaded, "Coach, I can kick the field goal."

With the rain beating down Shula signaled time out and turned to Garo and shouted, "God dammit! If you think you can do it go ahead and kick."

Garo ran onto the field praying as he went. He had second thoughts about his spur-of-the-moment promise to make the kick. This game was his last opportunity to prove that he was the man to be the DOLPHINS' kicker. His professional life was on the line. Karl Kremser's two week "move list" period would be over in a few more days.

Garo says, "My brain was in a state of suspension. I could see, hear, and feel but, there was no perception of reality."

During a high speed crash top race car drivers say that there is a feeling that everything is happening in slow motion. There is plenty of time to decide what to do.

The referee blew the whistle to start the play. Garo's brain was in a slow motion state. He knew exactly what he had to do. The ball was snapped. The holder placed it down, laces forward. Garo's perfectly timed approach, right leg plant and left leg swing blended into a marvelous instrument of football action. The ball left his toe and soared over the outstretched hands of the leaping Oakland RAIDERS' defensive linemen.

It traveled across the threshold of unbelief propelled by the rising roar from the largest crowd ever to gather in the Orange Bowl for a DOLPHINS regular game. Down the hallway of possibility the football found its way over the lonesome valley of rejection and cut through the rain and swirling winds passing the sentinels of hope into the realm of success. The ball cleared the bar squarely between the 21'6" separation of the goal posts.

The roar of the crowd reverberated throughout the stadium and the rain drops merged with the suddenly released tears in Garo's eyes. The half ended as his teammates surrounded him for wild congratulations. The score at half time, Miami 10-Oakland 3.

Karl Kremser, a sportsman and gentleman to the end, came over and shook hands and said, "Good job, Garo."

The rains ended and the field drained nicely during half time.

In the third quarter venerable George Blanda's kick added three more points to the Oakland score.

In the fourth quarter Paul Warfield made another sensational catch for Miami and Garo kicked the extra point-Miami 17-Oakland 6. Garo came on in the fourth quarter and made a 40-yard field goal for Miami's final score. Oakland's Warren Wells made a one-handed circus catch of a Daryl Lamonica pass for Oakland's lone touchdown with one minute left in the game. The final score was Miami 20-Oakland 13. The two Miami field goals were a vital part of the game.

The next day in the DOLPHINS locker room there was a note on Garo's locker that said, "Go see coach." In Pro Football that message usually foretells bad news.

Garo went into Shula's office and Don said, "Sit down, Garo. What is the longest kick you ever made?"

Garo, "47-yards."

Shula, "I know, that was last night. What was your longest before that?

Garo, "43-yards."

Shula, "I know that too. What made you think you could make a 47-yard field goal against the wind in an important game?"

"Coach, I'm very hungry and I need this job. I'll do whatever is necessary to stay with the team."

Shula, "Well, you don't have to worry about it. You've made the team. I released Karl Kremser. Another thing, I want to thank you for the way you won the job. I know that Karl Taseff was calling you every day during the strike. You stuck by your guns and didn't give in and won the job the right way. I have a lot of respect for you for that."

Karl Kremser was picked up by the Baltimore COLTS. He became a strong candidate to win the kicking job with Baltimore. He had bad luck with injuries and did not make the team. Eventually, he became the soccer coach for Florida International University.

Garo's life was destined to come to focus on another turning point in his life in the not too distant future.

Chapter 12 &

Vartan and Varteny Javian operated a Dry Cleaning business in Philadelphia. Through dedicated hard work their business grew from one small store to a chain of seventy-five ORIGINAL RAINBOW CLEANERS and DYERS, Inc.

They had been married for twenty-two years when Maritza Vart Javian was born. Their daughter was the light of their lives. An only child, Maritza became the center of their existence. She went to elementary and high school in Philadelphia's Quaker school system. Upon graduation she was accepted at all-girls Harcum Junior College in Bryn Mawr, Pennsylvania. Later, she transferred from Harcum to the University of Miami.

Maritza was quick to make friends as she pursued her studies for a degree in elementary education. One friend who knew of her Armenian heritage told Maritza that there was an Armenian kicker on the Miami DOLPHINS football team.

Maritza replied with a non-committal, "That's nice."

She had no brothers and didn't understand football. Soccer was the main sport of choice at her former Quaker schools. They did not field football teams.

About mid-October as she walked across the campus to attend an art class she heard the name Garo in her head. She couldn't understand why that name should be coming to mind. She knew a couple of Armenian boys in Philadelphia with that name but it made no sense to her that that name should occupy her thoughts.

The DOLPHINS had followed up their victory over the RAIDERS with a 20-6 victory over the New York JETS on Sunday, October 11th and the name Garo was being freely talked about in and around Miami. Maritza denies that she was aware of the DOLPHINS' success since the game of football meant nothing to her. The feeling passed and she went on to her class and had other things to think about.

A week later she got a phone call from a family friend who said that someone who had worked for her father wanted to see her. Maritza thought it was probably some older person who had retired to Florida.

On Wednesday evening, October 28th, Maritza's family friends were staging a grand opening of their son's CHICKEN UNLIMITED restaurant. Garo Yepremian, Doug Swift, Mercury Morris and Larry Little were scheduled to be there as representatives of the DOLPHINS. The family invited Maritza to bring her friends to come and meet the football players. She decided to go and invited one of the Armenian students who worked for the college radio station to go with her. He was excited about the opportunity for close contact with the DOLPHINS.

On the way to the grand opening the woman showed Maritza a large color picture of Garo in the Miami Herald. It showed Garo standing in the middle of the Orange Bowl wearing a jacket and tie. He had several neckties hanging around his neck and draped on his arm. A writer for the Miami Herald had picked up on the story of Garo the tie breaker being a tie maker.

Maritza thought, "He's has a nice smile and looks like a kind person."

When the group arrived at the restaurant a large crowd had gathered to meet the celebrities. The DOLPHINS defeated the Buffalo Bills 33-14 on Sunday, October 18th. Garo kicked four field goals in that game from 46-yards, 42-yards, 47-yards and 30-yards.

The game on the October 25th was a disappointment. The Cleveland BROWNS came to town and beat the DOLPHINS 28-0. The DOLPHINS quarterback, Bob Griese was booed. The fans were in deep frustration.

On one of Garo's field goal attempts the ball got loose. He picked it up and tried to run and was immediately tackled. He felt strange at the bottom of the pile and was lucky to be unhurt. The DOLPHINS fans are forgiving people. They were eager to meet the DOLPHIN players in person. Maritza sat in a booth with her friend and waited as the four players signed autographs. She had not been introduced to Garo. Maritza's cousin in Philadelphia was a dedicated autograph hound. When the crowd thinned out a little she decided to ask Garo for his autograph.

Garo said, "Who is this for."

She replied, "My cousin Leon, in Philadelphia."

Garo, "What is your name? I'll sign one for you, too."

"My name is Maritza Javian, thank you."

As Garo was writing he said, "I think my brother knows you."

She asked, "Who is your brother?"

He said, "Krikor Yepremian."

Maritza's father had been part owner of a hotel in Asbury Park, New Jersey in the mid-fifties. When Maritza was between the ages of six and ten years old her mother took her to the hotel during the summer months. During that time she and her mother met Krikor who had a summer job working at the hotel. He was fond of young Maritza and often took her shopping. She remembers the time when Krikor was ill and her mother took care of him until he got well.

At the end of that summer Krikor went back to continue his studies at Indiana University. That was the last time she saw Krikor. She would often ask her mother what happened to him. As her conversation with Garo continued she realized that he was indeed the brother of her long remembered childhood friend.

Maritza's friend asked Garo if he could interview him for the college radio station.

Garo said, "Sure. Give me your phone number and I will call you."

Maritza thought, "I hope that he asks for my phone number."

As she was hoping Garo said, "I might as well get your phone number, too."

She gave her phone number to him. After the ceremonies Garo smiled and waved good bye to her.

Maritza thought, "I hope he calls me."

On the way home her friends told her it was Krikor who had wanted her phone number. Krikor had come to Miami to see his brother play in the game against the Oakland RAIDERS on Saturday night, October 3rd. Krikor went back to Detroit before he had an opportunity to meet Maritza. She tried to block the memory of Garo out of her mind since she knew that he was very popular, very busy, and not likely to call her. She didn't want to be disappointed.

The following weekend the DOLPHINS played the Philadelphia EAGLES. The EAGLES dominated the first three quarter of the game. The DOLPHINS tried to make a close game out of it when Garo kicked a 24-yard field goal for their first score in the fourth quarter. The DOLPHINS followed up with two touchdowns but the final score was EAGLES 24-DOLPHINS 17.

On Monday, November 9th Maritza had a late class in elementary education. When she got back to her room her roommate wasn't there.

She went next door and another girl said, "Some guy called for you three times today. He wouldn't leave his name."

About that time Maritza heard the phone ringing in her room.

She ran and picked up the phone and said, "Hello."

The voice on the other end said, "Hello! Is Maritza there?

"This is she."

"This is Garo Yepremian. Do you remember me?"

"Of course I do."

"I know it's late but do you want to go out to dinner?"

"Yes, I'll go with you"

Garo arrived in his yellow Pontiac Bonneville with a landau roof and told her they would go to the STUDIO RESTAURANT. When they got there they found that the STUDIO RESTAURANT was closed. He circled and went back to THE PUB RESTAU-RANT in Coral Gables, Florida. After a short wait they were seated and Maritza wondered what she should order since the prices seemed rather high.

Garo saw her looking at the right side of the menu and said, "When you have dinner with me don't look at the prices."

She remembered that her father said the same thing when the family went out to dinner. She ordered prime rib and Garo had the same.

Garo blames the pressure of big time football for playing games with his mind that caused him to criticize Maritza on their first date. He didn't like the way she wore her long curly hair. He complained about the fringes on her handbag. He said it made her look like a hippie especially since she was wearing sandals. He thought her dress was too old fashioned. Maritza kept her thoughts to herself even though Garo looked a little wild in his paisley shirt and flowered tie.

Garo told her that he had spent six years in London before coming to the United States.

Maritza thought, "At least he's not a boat job."

Often, when young Armenian men arrived in the

United States the Armenian families would introduce them to eligible girls. In casual conversation the girls giggled and called the new arrivals "boat jobs."

Garo must not have been too disappointed with Maritza.

He looked at her sandals and said, "You have very pretty toes."

After dinner they went for a ride.

Usually when she went out on a date Maritza wondered how she could get out of kissing her date goodnight. When she looked at Garo she found herself wishing that he would kiss her. Garo must have read her mind. They stopped at a traffic light and Garo leaned over and kissed Maritza.

He said, "I'm sorry I complained about your dress. Would you go out with me tomorrow night?"

She answered, "Yes."

They arrived at Maritza's dormitory about thirty minutes before her eleven o'clock curfew.

When Maritza got out of the car Garo spoke of himself using an indefinite pronoun.

He said, "I think someone likes you."

She smiled and waved good night. As she turned away her long hair swirled around her shoulders.

Garo thought, "I must be nuts. Her hair is beautiful when the light shines on it."

During the next day's session with the previous Sunday's game films Garo daydreamed about the soft spoken, dark-haired, Maritza. His concentration was definitely not on football.

That evening Garo picked Maritza up at six o'clock and they went to radio station WGBS to meet Bob Sheridan. Bob took them to a boxing show. Jimmy

Ellis was fighting another heavyweight in the main event. Their seats were near the front row. The pounding punches splashed blood and sweat in their direction. Close up, Maritza thought that boxing was a brutal sport and from what she knew about it football was much the same.

Garo returned Maritza to her dorm.

Before she got out of the car he said, "The public relations man for Richard's department store in Miami has arranged an appearance for me and some other DOLPHINS. Will you go with me to the store tomorrow evening?"

Maritza said, "That would be nice."

His parting words to Maritza again contained an indefinite pronoun.

He said, "I know somebody likes you."

He sang to himself all the way home.

The next evening while Garo was signing autographs at Richard's Maritza passed the time by going shopping. Garo said to the store's promotion man, "See that girl coming down the escalator, I am going to marry her. She doesn't know it, yet."

The great Garo Yepremian the man who had dodged the conniving efforts of scores of Armenian parents who attempted to get him to take an interest in their eligible daughters; the man who had avoided any lasting love entanglements was a helpless lump of love stricken clay in the company of Maritza Javian.

Top-of-the-chart love songs and an uncountable number of poems, novels, movies and television shows haven't been able to completely define the magic that glows when love's lightning bolt strikes.

After the autograph party Garo shook hands with

the promotion man and left the store to drive Maritza home. Once again he made a date to pick her up the next night.

On their fourth date while they were driving through the city Garo shouted, "I'm gonna marry you."

Maritza, "Do you know what you are saying?"

Garo, "I know what I'm saying. Do you know what I'm saying?"

A few weeks earlier Maritza had a conversation with one of her favorite aunts about how to tell when you are in love.

Her aunt said, "You'll just know. You won't have to ask anyone."

Maritza's feelings about Garo were different than any she had experienced before. On their first date, just four days earlier, she had hoped that Garo would kiss her and that was so different than her usual thoughts. After only four dates with this wonderful man she knew that she was in love.

Maritza said, "Yes, I know what you are saying. Yes, OK! I will marry you."

Garo drove his yellow Pontiac Bonneville with the landau roof over to the curb and took Maritza in his arms. Their tears of joy mingled as his mouth found hers. When their love-sealing kiss ended they talked and giggled in a rush of emotion. Garo repeated the words "I love you" and kissed her several times to erase the strangeness out of them. The more he said those words the sweeter the sound. They talked about how they would tell their parents and friends about their agreement to marry. For the time being since everything had happened so fast they decided not to tell anyone.

The DOLPHINS were scheduled to play the Atlanta FALCONS in the Orange Bowl on the upcoming Sunday. Krikor, his son Sarko and brother Berj were flying into Miami to see the game. Garo and Maritza went to the airport to meet the plane.

Krikor was happy to see Maritza and they talked about the summers in Asbury Park at her father's hotel.

On Sunday, November 22nd, Krikor, Berj and Maritza sat in the stands to watch the game. Maritza and Garo had arranged a set of signs for communication. She would wave an orange scarf and when Garo saw it he would slap his helmet two times. He knew the general area where she was seated. It only took him a few minutes to locate her and send back the confirming signal. Maritza had several opportunities to cheer.

With quarterback Bob Griese leading the attack the DOLPHINS scored two touchdowns and Garo completed two extra point kicks. He also kicked a 43-yard field goal followed by a successful 9-yard one.

Maritza was hoarse from all of the cheering. Krikor thought she was a football crazy fan. Little did he know that she really didn't understand the game very well and that her cheers were for a very special person.

Miami won the game 20-7 over the FALCONS.

The following Thursday was Thanksgiving and Maritza left Miami to go home to Philadelphia for the holiday break. Of course, when she got home she showed Garo's picture to her parents and told them how she met him and how she had managed to meet their old friend Krikor.

Maritza's Dad didn't believe that a young girl college student should go steady. He was feeling the normal pangs of jealousy that a father experiences when some strange man threatens to take away his only daughter. He had heard stories about professional athletes and their wild ways. He feared that his beloved daughter would become just another stop along the way for an ego driven professional football player.

Maritza was so lonesome in Philadelphia knowing that Garo was faraway in Miami. Her father's confusion and heartbreak was compounded when Maritza decided to return to Miami on Friday after Thanksgiving. He moped around the house all weekend. When he went to work on Monday he sat in his office with his head in his hands.

One of his employees said, "Boss, are you okay?

The "boss" was certainly not himself that week. He felt sad and depressed.

That evening Maritza's Mom said, "I think we should go to Miami and meet Garo."

Maritza received the call from her Mom saying that they were coming to Miami. She told Garo about the coming visit. Garo immediately called his parents and told them to come to Miami to meet his new girl friend.

Maritza's parents were booked in at the Holiday Inn and Garo's parents were to stay at his place. The first evening that the parents were in Miami arrangements were made for a get together at the Holiday Inn.

Maritza's parents liked Garo and were pleased with his manners and outgoing nature. Sarkis and Azadouhi immediately fell in love with Maritza. The parents agreed that it was good that Garo and Maritza had found each other. They began to make plans for an engagement party in Philadelphia. The party would follow the Armenian tradition. The parents then joined in an Armenian custom and made a promissory toast.

They touched glasses and Maritza's father said, "Let's drink to our kids and their future."

The whole party went to the STUDIO RESTAURANT and enjoyed a nice evening of food and conversation. Vartan Javian would never again worry about losing his daughter. He truly felt that he was gaining a son. He thought Garo was a wonderful fellow.

The Boston PATRIOTS were scheduled to play the DOLPHINS on Sunday, Dec. 6th. The families made plans to see the game.

Maritza asked her mother about the Armenian custom wherein the girl to be engaged was given a piece of jewelry. Her mother told her that the boy's parents usually presented the gift. That Sunday before the game Azadouhi slipped two gold bracelets on Maritza's arm. That gesture told her that she had been accepted by Garo's parents.

The DOLPHINS beat the PATRIOTS 37-20. Mercury Morris ran the opening kick-off back for a touchdown and Garo kicked three field goals from fifteen, thirty-nine and twenty yards. Vartan didn't understand the rules of the game. He managed to have a good laugh that day when buxom Morgana ran onto the field. Morgana had become dubiously famous for showing up at public events. She usually ran onto the playing area to kiss and official or a player.

When Vartan returned to Philadelphia he asked a neighbor girl to come to the house and watch football on television and explain the game to him.

The DOLPHINS were on a roll. On December 13th, they beat the New York JETS 16 to 10. Garo made three field goals from 40, 14 and 21 yards. The last two came in the final two minutes of the game. The crowd went wild and the newspaper reporters started calling him Miami's bald-headed marvel.

A pregnant woman in Fort Lauderdale said that she was going to name her new baby Garo because it kicked so hard.

Garo was very happy at this time. He had found Maritza and was playing for a coach that he admired. Unlike his days with the Detroit LIONS, his teammates respected him and he respected them.

Garo became a favorite with the writers and broadcasters. He was ever ready to give an interview and usually had a good quip or two to insert into the conversation. He usually stayed in the locker room until the last reporter had and opportunity to talk to him. Garo enjoyed the spotlight. He was still the little boy who had grabbed a flag and strutted in the political parade in Larnaca, Cyprus.

The DOLPHINS finished their regular season by beating the Buffalo BILLS in a 47-7 rout. They were playoff bound and would play the Oakland RAIDERS in the Oakland Coliseum on Sunday, December 27th. The team and the Miami fans were happy to be going to the playoffs.

On game day the Coliseum was a mud hole. The rains had been heavy and the natural turf was sodden. Some of the DOLPHIN players think that the RAIDERS owner, Al Davis, instructed the ground crew to pump extra water on the field to slow the game even further. That rumor is unsubstantiated and may have been only locker room talk. The RAIDERS beat the DOLPHINS 21-14 in what the Miami team and their supporters called the mud bowl.

The fans thought that the DOLPHINS first year under the guidance of Don Shula was a success.

After his playing days with the BROWNS, COLTS and REDSKINS Shula had been a defensive aid with the Detroit LIONS. In 1963 the Baltimore COLTS fired Weeb Ewbank and Don Shula replaced him as head coach of the COLTS. Ewbank went on to become the coach of the New York JETS. In 1969, Weeb took the JETS to Miami to play the COLTS in the Super Bowl. Weeb got his revenge. Joe Namath became a legend because he guaranteed a JETS victory although the COLTS were listed as a seventeen point favorite by "Jimmy the Greek." Jimmy set the betting line for the Las Vegas casinos. The JETS won 16-7 and brought the American Football League into parity with the National Football League.

Don Shula left the COLTS and became the head coach of the Miami DOLPHINS in 1970.

He assembled a group composed of a few veteran players, some draft choices, and several castoffs from other teams. They made it to the playoffs with a young team and were in position to have a good season in 1971. In Shula's mind this was not good enough. He'd had the experience of losing a Super Bowl game and would not be satisfied with anything less than a Super Bowl victory by his team.

A coach does not become a legend without dreams. Don Shula is a dreamer and master psychologist. He makes his dreams contagious and infects all of his players with the idea that they can play far beyond their individual athletic ability. He had done a good job on Garo and Garo responded by performing beyond his expected reach.

1970 was the first year that the player's names were put on the back of their jerseys and Garo wore his with pride.

In 1970, the National Football League was organized into two conferences. The American Conference and the National Conference each had thirteen teams and three divisions-Eastern, Central and Western. Miami was in the Eastern Division of the American Conference. The Miami DOLPHINS greatest years were yet to come.

During the winter of 1971 Garo and Maritza continued their intensive courtship and love for each other. Garo made many personal appearances and talked to his fans on a daily radio show.

On January 30th there was an engagement party at Maritza'a home in Philadelphia. The Very Reverend Zaven Arzoumanian and The Very Reverend Father Yeghishe Ghizirian, now a Bishop in London, conducted the formal engagement ceremony. Rings were exchanged and the wedding date was set for June 12, 1971. Everyone cried for joy.

Garo and Maritza returned to Miami. Maritza went into the second semester at the University of Miami. Maritza went home for the Easter break. After a few days Garo flew up to Philadelphia to be with her. He couldn't stand the separation.

In late May and early June Garo fulfilled his army reserve obligation by serving two weeks at Camp Blanding, Florida, with Headquarters Company, First Battalion, of the 24th Infantry Division. His picture in the paper looked a little funny since he was dressed in a white army cook's outfit while demonstrating his kicking prowess. He was considered to be a good sports story by the radio, TV and press in South Florida. The fans loved it.

On June 12th, at 4:00 p.m., the wedding was held at Holy Trinity Armenian Church in Cheltenham, Pennsylvania. Archbishop Torkom Manoogian, the man who had baptized Maritza, was in attendance. He is now the Patriarch of Jerusalem. Father Ghizirian and The Very Reverend Father Zaven Arzoumanian the priest at Holy Trinity church also were members of the attending clergy.

Bob Sheridan arranged to announce the wedding on radio station WGBS in Miami. By coincidence Tricia Nixon Cox's wedding was on television at the same time.

Gabriel Soultanian, Garo's godfather who originally came over from Cyprus and was now living in Chicago was the Best Man. Hilda, his wife was Matron of Honor. Garo's brothers Berj, Krikor and Maritza's cousins Leon and Mickey were ushers. Leon was the cousin for whom Maritza asked Garo to sign an autograph on the day they first met at Chicken Unlimited in Florida. Tina, a family friend was flower girl and little Sarko was the ring bearer.

There was no air conditioning in the church and everyone was sweating. Maritza prepared to walk down the aisle. Her cousin announced that the organ was broken but that the chimes were still working. The organist played the Wedding March on the chimes. The bride was beautiful in her flowing white gown. Garo and the Best Man arrived at the altar. Garo was nervous. He was accustomed to large crowds and pushy reporters but this was something different.

The bride and groom put rings on at the beginning of the ceremony and crowns were placed on their heads to symbolize that they were King and Queen for the day. They put their heads together and the Best Man held a cross over them while the priests intoned their solemn prayers. Their vows were given and the wedding ended. The party went to the Marriott Inn on City Line in Philadelphia for the reception. An Armenian band from New York and a local Armenian band provided the music. Vartan Javian made sure that his beloved daughter entered into marriage in fine style.

Music, lots of food, many fine gifts and a lot of hand shaking, kissing and backslapping occurred. Garo was proud and happy for the most part.

Strange as it seems, Garo showed the jealous side of his personality. He didn't want Maritza to dance with the other men. He didn't like it when her garter was thrown to the crowd. During the four years he had been playing professional football there was always someone threatening to take his job. He had met con artists who wanted to use his name in various business enterprises. He had become very defensive in nature and possessive of his achievements. It wasn't that he doubted Maritza's fidelity it was just part of the defense mechanism that he developed to insulate himself from the heartbreak of rejection.

Maritza, too, had to accept the attention that Garo received from female members of the public. It went with the territory when you were married to a star player in the National Football League. Yes, she has had jealous moments. However, her jealousy and

Garo's possessiveness has never been a real problem. After more than twenty years of marriage they are still in the hand holding and kissy face state of romance.

They went on a honeymoon to Acapulco and Mexico City. When they returned Garo weighed one-hundred-and-eighty-seven pounds. He was overweight and needed to get down to one-hundred-and-seventy pounds. He started running and went on a diet because training camp would be starting soon. He didn't relish undergoing Shula's exercise regimen carrying extra pounds.

His contract for 1971 was to include a ten-percent increase over his 1970 salary. That would be $14,300 for the season. He didn't want to sign the contract. He was the leading kicker in the league and thought he was worth much more than that. Krikor negotiated hard for him.

Joe Thomas, the business manager said, "Take it or leave it."

Don Shula begged Garo, "Please sign. I don't want to lose you. You are a good kicker. If you have a good year I'll help you get more money in 1972"

Garo gave in and signed the contract.

Maritza's mother and girl friend came to Florida to stay with her while Garo was in training camp.

The DOLPHINS brought in a straight on kicker from Stanford University in California. Steve Horowitz was a 220-pounder who had kicked two field goals in the 1971 Rose Bowl game. One of the kicks was a 48-yarder that helped Stanford upset Ohio State 27-17. Horowitz had set a lot of records at Stanford and the nationally televised Rose Bowl game opened many doors for him. When Steve Horowitz saw Garo making his practice kicks at training camp he knew he was in trouble.

Paul Kaplan, in the Miami News, quoted him saying, "Picking Miami was like sending a free agent quarterback to compete against Roman Gabriel or John Brodie."

Those were two of the outstanding quarterbacks in the league.

Horowitz went on to say, "I guess my agent didn't know that Yepremian was the best kicker in the NFL last year."

Don Shula retained bad memories about the field conditions during the playoff game at Oakland the previous season. He wanted Garo to get some experience kicking in bad field conditions. A sand box was constructed so that the coaches could duplicate extreme field problems. Once each week Garo was required to practice in the "sand box."

Jake Scott and Garo were the last two players signed for the year.

Joe Robbie managing partner of the team said, "Garo signed for a salary that puts him on a level with other good kickers in pro football."

Krikor and Garo didn't agree with that statement. They thought that since he was the best kicker in the league the year before he deserved more than a ten percent increase in his minimum league salary of $13,000.

During this period the newspaper writers made a big thing out of Garo's necktie business. He started that necktie business out of desperation when he was cut by Detroit. His Mom made them by hand and that was a slow process. His picture in the Miami Herald with his neckties helped the story along.

Dick Anderson played safety for the Dolphins. He was always looking for a way to make an extra dollar. Following his years as a football player he became a Florida state Senator and a scratch golfer. He suggested to Garo that they go into business and put Garo's ties in stores in Florida. They approached Burdine's Department store and talked to one of the top managers. He called in the haberdashery buyer and the buyer got excited about the proposition. He gave Garo and Dick and order for 320 dozen neckties at six dollars per tie. The ties would be sold in eight Florida stores. Garo agreed to supply two players in each store on a Monday night to sign autographs.

The next problem was how were they going to get the ties made. Garo's Mom could turn out about two dozen per week. That was way to slow to fill the order they had in hand. They looked in the phone book for sewing factory listings. After a few calls, they found a company in Pompano Beach that had a warehouse full of neckties. That was Lyons Neckwear. They entered the building and saw thousands of neckties of many colors. Neckties were everywhere.

Mr. Lyons pushed Garo to an area of the warehouse where he had an assortment of wild ties.

Garo and Dick realized the Mr. Lyons was ready to sell when he said, "I have 800 dozen. I want two-dollars for each tie."

Garo said, "We'll take all of them if you will put a label in each tie that says it is an original by Garo Yepremian and a little set of goal posts with a dolphin jumping through it. And by the way, we will need to have them delivered to Miami."

Mr. Lyons said, "It's a deal."

When the 800 dozen ties were delivered there were eight dozen ties of the same color in each box. The boxes filled the two-and-a-half car garage at Garo's house. Garo and Maritza sorted the ties by hand and mixed several colors in each box. They then delivered the ties to the eight Burdine's department stores.

Garo made a deal with Mercury Morris, his buddy Doug Swift, Manny Fernandez, Jim Kiick, Marv Fleming just to name a few. The players were to be paid $50.00 each to go to a department store for two hours on Monday evening and sign autographs. The ties sold for $12.00 in the stores. The players were given the option to take a dozen ties or fifty dollars for their pay. Most of the players opted to take the ties. It wasn't too long before Dick Anderson tired of the tie deal. He dropped out of the tie business. It took Garo a couple of years to get rid of the remaining ties. The publicity generated by the tie business helped the tie maker-tie breaker legend continue to grow.

The 1971 season opened for Miami at Mile High stadium in Denver. The game against the BRONCOS ended in a 10-10 tie. The DOLPHINS fumbled four times and Garo missed three field goals. His attempts from the 45, 36 and 35 yard lines were disasters in his mind. The BRONCOS and the DOLPHINS both played sloppy games. Garo was in a depressed state of mind. He thought his performance was awful.

Don Shula gave the team a special speech in which he said, "Put it behind you and move ahead. We still believe in you."

Garo felt certain that the fans in Miami would be angry. He got a surprising amount of good mail that week. There was one negative letter writer. The fan drew a 10-10 on the letter and printed "We didn't buy a tie like this."

Shoes have always been an important part of Garo's kicking game. He normally wears size 8 1/2 shoes for street use. He wears a 7 1/2 shoe on his left foot during a game. He was wearing a new pair in the Denver game because his old shoes were pretty well worn.

During the week while he was shopping a group of kids came up to him and asked for autographs.

He thought, "Those kids still think I'm okay."

Garo says that when others have confidence in you it help you have confidence in yourself.

On the following Sunday the DOLPHINS played the Buffalo BILLS on a damp, chilly, overcast day at War Memorial Stadium in Buffalo. The DOLPHINS rebounded from their tie with Denver. They defeated the BILLS 29-14. It was a total team effort. Larry Czonka and Jim Kiick each ran for more than a hundred yards. Czonka suffered a broken nose in the game and continued to play with blood running down his face. He reported that it was the ninth time his nose had been broken. He was one tough football player.

Garo scored on five field goals ranging from 15 yards to 48-yards. Two of those field goals were from 43-yards. That was a team record for the number of field goals in one game. Bob DeMarco was the DOLPHINS center and Karl Noonan was the holder.

The editorial board of Pro Football Weekly voted Garo the Thom McAn Shoe Company's weekly

Golden Toe Award. And by the way, he was wearing his old shoes in the Buffalo game. He didn't replace his shoes until a new pair arrived from Germany later in the season.

Under Don Shula's coaching, the DOLPHINS were rounding into shape. They went through the season with a strong Czonka/Kiick rushing game and the breakaway running of Mercury Morris. Bob Griese was a masterful quarterback whose passing to Paul Warfield and others helped keep the game open for the running attack. Garo had an excellent season. He connected on 28 out of 40 field goals. He was deadly accurate inside the 30-yard line. He had no misses from that distance. He finished the regular season with 117 points to lead the league in scoring.

The DOLPHINS and the Kansas City CHIEFS ended the regular season with identical records, 10 wins-3 losses and 1 tie.

The CHIEFS and the DOLPHINS were scheduled for a playoff game on Christmas day 1971.

Pete Rozelle and the NFL were criticized by some for scheduling the game on Christmas. Saturday, December 25th, 1971 saw a record breaking 63 degrees on the thermometer at game time 3:00 P.M. Eastern Standard Time.

One protester carried a sign in front of Kansas City's Municipal Stadium that said, "Are you PRO-CHRIST or ANTI-CHRIST?"

In spite of the protest 50,374 fans arrived to make it a capacity crowd. Standing room only tickets were made available. The game was to be televised to a national audience on NBC-TV.

After a short workout the day before Don Shula

said, "The weather is just beautiful and the turf is in good condition."

The veteran grounds keeper, George Toma had kept the field covered every night since Thanksgiving. He removed the cover in the daytime. George was proud of the field conditions and was optimistic about his teams chances.

DOLPHINS quarterback, Bob Griese had missed the previous game. He injured his shoulder in the Monday night game against the Chicago BEARS on November 29th. Paul Warfield, his favorite receiver was suffering from bruised ribs received in the game against the Green Bay PACKERS on the preceding Sunday.

Hank Stram, the CHIEFS coach, worried about the deep threat posed by Paul Warfield coupled with the breakaway running of Mercury Morris and the rushing game of Larry Czonka and Jim Kiick. Len Dawson, the CHIEFS quarterback had been off for a week. Stram was worried about his timing.

In the season rankings the DOLPHINS were second in total offense, first in rushing and 10th in passing. They were second in overall defense, fourth against the rush and fourth against the pass.

On the other side, the CHIEFS were fifth in total offense, seventh in rushing and third in passing, third in total defense, second against the rush and twelfth against the pass.

On Friday before the game, the DOLPHINS learned that Jan Stenerud had been selected by the AFC coaches to go to the Pro-Bowl game. The team thought that Garo should have been the one selected for that honor.

Jan Stenerud had been on the ski jumping team at

Montana State. He came over from Fetsund, Norway where skiing is the national passion. He was an excellent ski jumper and brought three NCAA titles to Montana State. He met his wife Lani at Montana State. She took him to football games even though he didn't understand what was happening on the field.

One day on his daily running workout he saw some friends kicking a football on the practice field. Jan joined them and discovered that he was a natural for football. Montana State lost a ski jumper and gained a football kicker. During the 1971 pro football season Jan made twenty-six out of forty-four field goal attempts. Garo notched twenty-eight out of forty. He was undeniably disappointed when he failed to be voted into the Pro Bowl game. It added a little bit of drama to the already exciting playoff struggle. While warming up for the game Garo went over and congratulated Stenerud for making the Pro Bowl team.

At game time, the Kansas City CHIEFS were three point favorites on the betting line.

The first quarter went as expected. The wily veteran, thirty-six year old Len Dawson flipped a seven yard pass to Ed Podolak who went in for the touchdown. An extra point by Jan Stenerud and the score was 7-0. Later in the quarter, Stenerud hit a 24 yard field goal. At the end of the quarter the score was CHIEFS 10-DOLPHINS 0.

In the second quarter the Miami defense stood its ground and the offense moved down the field. Larry Czonka scored on a one-yard plunge. Garo kicked the extra point-score DOLPHINS 7-CHIEFS 10. Before half-time Garo tied the score with a kick from the 14-yard line. Kansas City missed an opportunity with

3:45 left in the half when Stenerud missed wide with a twenty-nine yard field goal attempt.

In the third quarter Len Dawson engineered a nine-minute drive capped by a one yard run by Jim Otis. Jan Stenerud kicked the extra point and the CHIEFS led 17-10.

Bob Griese and the DOLPHINS came right back with an eight play seventy-three yard drive followed by a Jim Kiick one yard plunge. Garo hit the extra point-tie score 17-17.

In the fourth quarter a sixty-three yard pass from Dawson to Elmo Wright set up a three-yard touchdown run by Ed Podolak. The Stenerud extra point put the CHIEFS in the lead 24-17.

After the kickoff, Griese took the DOLPHINS offense on a nine-play series for seventy-one yards. On the next play he flipped the ball to Marv Fleming who powered his way for five yards to make the touchdown. Garo tied the score with his extra point conversion. The DOLPHINS had come from behind for the third time to tie the score. There was 1:36 left in the game.

Garo kicked off and the Kansas City fans went wild as victory seemed in their grasp. Ed Podolak took the kickoff and raced up the middle of the field. He cut back to his left and went down the sideline. Garo was the only player between Podolak and a clear run to pay dirt. DOLPHIN defensive back Curtis Johnson came over and drove Podolak out of bounds on the DOLPHINS 22-yard line.

Later Ed said, "I had to slow down a little to dodge him (Garo) and somebody hit me from the other side."

The fans were in a frenzy. Jan Stenerud strode in from the sidelines to make what was for him a routine three point kick. The ball was placed down thirty-three yards from the crossbar. There were :35 seconds left in the game. Stenerud's kick was up and away. None of the surging defensive players were able to get a hand on it. Unbelievably, the ball failed to hook in and stayed out to the right missing the goalpost by inches. The crowd was stunned when the great opportunity for victory slipped from their hands.

The DOLPHINS took possession on their twenty yard line. They were unable to make a first down and the ball was punted away. The CHIEFS receiver signaled for a fair catch as time ran out. According to league rules, if a team ended the game with a fair catch they were entitled to make a free kick. It would have been a 68-yard attempt for Stenerud. If he failed to reach the goal line with the kick the DOLPHINS would have had the opportunity to run it back. Common sense told Coach Hank Stram that it was foolhardy to try for a 68-yard field goal. He elected to let the regulation game end in a 24-24 tie and go into an overtime period.

It was so exciting that backfield judge Adrian Burk turned to a group of people on the sideline and said, "This is one 'helluva' football game."

Len Dawson won the coin flip for the CHIEFS. After 3:45 of playing time the CHIEFS were in position for a 42-yard field goal attempt. The teams lined up. The tired muscles of the DOLPHINS defensive unit tensed in a superhuman effort to avert a loss in this crucial contest. The ball was snapped and placed down perfectly. Stenerud hit it on the nose.

When the ball sailed over the DOLPHINS defensive line middle linebacker Nick Bouniconti leaped and got a hand on the flying football. There was no score. The remainder of the fifth period was a classic defensive exhibition by both teams. The DOLPHINS had another opportunity with 2:49 left in the first overtime period. Garo missed on a 52-yard attempt that was wide of the mark. Shula was desperately seizing any chance that might produce a score in sudden death play. The determination, iron will and hard-nosed body contact kept the fans in a continuous state of excitement. They were watching football history in the making.

After a two minute rest, the teams began the second overtime period. The DOLPHINS had the ball on their own 30-yard line after a Kansas City punt. Bob Griese handed the ball off to Jim Kiick who went into the line for a five yard gain. It was now second and five. Due to the length of the game most of the DOLPHINS plays had been well-used. It was time for Bob Griese to pull something out of the hat. He called for a draw play with Czonka carrying the ball. On the snap of the ball Griese handed the ball to Czonka who turned and went against the flow of the play. There were many highly technical blocking assignments on that play and it caught the CHIEFS unprepared. Czonka broke through for twenty-nine yards to the CHIEFS 36-yard line. As play continued Kiick went into the line for two yards and Czonka gained four on second down. Jim Kiick was unable to gain yardage on third down. However, he had the presence of mind to get the ball down squarely in front of the goal posts. And there it was—Garo's golden opportunity.

With the LIONS in 1966 he had reacted to his own physical fears and broke the record for the most field goals in a single game. Those field goals proved to him that he had what it takes to compete in the NFL. The 47-yard kick that he made in a tropical downpour in Miami in 1970 was done out of desperation because he had to make the team. Here in Kansas City in 1971 he was eager to do his best for the team.

Garo said, "I watched my teammates give their all to reach that position on the field and I didn't intend to let them down."

Center Mike Kolen snapped the ball and Karl Noonan put it down for the 37-yard kick. Don Shula stood on the sideline with his arms folded across his chest and a grim jut-jawed look on his face. Garo went to the ball with his left foot. A hushed silence came over the stadium.

Garo says, "When the ball left my instep I turned my face skyward and thanked God for giving me the opportunity to make that kick. I knew it was good the instant it left my foot."

After 22-minutes-and-forty-seconds of overtime play the ball sailed through the goal posts and the longest game in pro football history was in the record books. The pictures of number 89, Karl Noonan, leaping high in the air with Garo being pummeled by his teammates and Don Shula doing what was later called the Shula Hula, as he lost his rigid game composure, were flashed around the nation.

The DOLPHINS defeated the CHIEFS 27-24. It was the first time all day that the DOLPHINS went into the lead.

In the post game interviews Don Shula said, "It is

the greatest victory I've been associated with. It was a victory that took guts and determination. My boys never quit. We've never won a bigger game."

The CHIEFS coach Hank Stram said, "It was fantastic, an unbelievable game."

DOLPHINS team owner Joe Robbie said, "This game should go into a highlights film about the history of football."

Pro football players play for money. That's part of the game. They also play for pride and self-fulfillment.

Ed Podolak cried in the CHIEFS locker room. He carried the ball seventeen times for eighty-five yards and had scored two touchdowns. Collectively, returning kickoffs punts and catching passes he had a total of 350 yards on offense. He played his heart out and the emotional letdown brought on the tears.

In the DOLPHINS locker room Larry Czonka threw up. Even in victory his emotions were truly spent.

The victory was sweet for the DOLPHINS and their fans. For the Kansas City CHIEFS and their fans it was a bitter defeat.

Jan Stenerud was one of the premier place kickers in the league and had carved a firm niche in the sport.

Garo said, "I understand Jan's feelings. I, too, had suffered in the opening game of the season where my inability to make the field goals caused the DOLPHINS to play to a tie with the Denver BRONCOS. I know it's a sad day for Jan."

Somewhere in the stadium, wherever team owners go in times of sadness, Lamar Hunt knew he would have to cancel the big half-time show he planned for the following week's game.

The media enjoyed a field day analyzing the reasons for Stenerud's ineffective kicking and all of the other plays and breaks of the game. In the long-range view of history there were no losers in that game. One team had to come out of it with the highest score and so it was the DOLPHINS. The individuals who gave everything they had to offer were football heroes on both sides of the score. The margin of victory was very thin indeed. The game and the players live on in football lore.

There was bedlam in the DOLPHINS locker room. Garo was the last one to take a shower. He had been busy giving out interviews to the media people.

The team was taken to the airport on buses. When they boarded the plane there were several cases of Mateus wine on the aircraft. When they were airborne and the seat belt sign went off instead of drinking it the players began pouring the wine on each other. The non-stop celebration lasted for two hours until they arrived over Miami. Later, it was determined that the plane had suffered thirty-five or forty thousand dollars in damage. The seats were stained and wine was in all of the crevices. The floor of the plane was wet with wine. On final approach to the airport one of the players looked out of the window and saw that there were fire engines down there with flashing lights. Garo was nervous. He hated flying.

Maritza knew when the team plane was due to arrive at the airport. She planned to meet Garo. Driving to the terminal she saw a lot of traffic. She thought that a major movie star must be arriving in Miami.

She asked a policeman, "What's happening?"

He said, "The DOLPHINS won."

Maritza replied, "Yes, I know. My husband won the game for them."

The policeman asked, "Are you Mrs. Yepremian?"

"Yes I am," she said.

The officer directed her to a diplomatic consul's parking spot. She fought her way through the crowd to get to the arrival gate. The police had stretched a rope to make a pathway for the players to walk through the terminal. It was a futile effort.

When the game ended the Miami fans saw the DOLPHINS victory on television. They started heading for the airport to greet the victorious team. The number of fans there that night has been estimated to be as many as twenty-five thousand. The police could not control the crowd. The security men surrounded Garo and escorted him through the mass of people. The happy fans were trying to touch him. Many were slapping at his bald head and some tried to rip his clothes to get a souvenir.

At the first corridor in the terminal building he saw Maritza and pulled her to his side. The police managed to get them to the police station on the lower level.

They said, "We'll stay here until the crowd thins out."

After a time, they made an announcement on the PA system, "Garo Yepremian has left the airport."

While Maritza and Garo were waiting in the police station a gentleman walked in carrying two bottles of champagne. He was introduced as Mr. Maytag, President of National Airlines. He was a member of the family that made the famous Maytag washing machines.

At 4:30 in the morning they were able to leave the

terminal building and go to their car. Garo arrived at his home at 5:30am. He drove down his home street. He saw paint on the street. People had decorated his entire house with signs that said, GARO IS #1, GARO IS OUR HERO, etc. Marty Bystrom was one of the boys who helped decorate Garo's house. Marty went on to become a pitcher in the major leagues. His career included a stint with the Philadelphia Phillies.

Garo and Maritza let the signs stay up for about two weeks. People would stop by the house and Garo would sign autographs and pose for pictures with the fans. He cut a pretty fancy figure with his long mutton chop sideburns.The sports media had a field day writing and talking about the "longest game."

Garo says with a chuckle, "That's when I learned why they called it sudden death overtime. The guys told me that if I had missed they were gonna kill me. Afterwards they said they were only joking, but I'm not so sure. It really was a team effort. We were a team all year. Everything we did, we did forty guys as one. When I made that field goal, the fans gave me the credit but the defense gave us the ball and the line blocked for me. They all were part of it, too."

Garo's remarks were a tribute to Shula's total-team psychology. In Detroit he felt like an outsider only barely tolerated as a team member. In Miami he was one of forty important parts that combined to make up the whole team.

Life is strange-Fate is fickle. It strikes in the strangest places. When Don Shula and his son finally got to their car they found that the battery was dead. The mighty Don Shula had to bum a ride home on one of his greatest days.

The next day, Sunday, December 26th, the Baltimore COLTS defeated the Cleveland BROWNS to set the league championship game in Miami on Sunday January 2nd, 1972. Don Shula was worried about the amount of time and energy being spent by the team and the fans celebrating the victory. His sights were on the Super Bowl. Baltimore was not to be taken lightly. Johnny Unitas, Bubba Smith and the other renowned COLTS has amassed impressive credentials over the years. By Wednesday Shula had the team back in focus.

Garo says, "Shula fretted and yelled at us. He said we would be nobodies if we let Baltimore beat us in front of our hometown fans and on national television. He reminded us that Baltimore sweated and worked hard to reach the championship game. They were hungry. There would be only one winner. If we expected to be the one we'd better forget about past glory and concentrate on the forthcoming game. His talk brought us back to earth. The guys started hitting hard and yelling at each other. You could feel desire building up in the team."

The COLTS were a one point favorite on the strength of the return to active duty of their great running backs Tom Matte and Norm Bulaich. Matte had been out with a bruised right knee and Bulaich was troubled with a hamstring pull. The COLTS defense was stingy and allowed only one-hundred-and-forty points to be scored against them in the regular season. Bubba Smith was their big man and the sports media called the defense Bubba and Company.

In the first quarter Paul Warfield scored for Miami

on a 75-yard pass play from Bob Griese. In the fourth quarter Dick Anderson made an interception and after five spectacular blocks by his teammates he went in for Miami's second score-Miami 14-Baltimore 0. Late in the fourth quarter Griese and Warfield connected on a 50-yard pass play and Larry Czonka took it in from the five. The game ended and the DOLPHINS had shut out the COLTS 21-0. It was a big day for Miami's overpowering offense but the big story was the tremendous effort put out by the DOLPHINS "No Name Defense." They were flawless in their shutout of a fine COLTS team.

This team that caused Danny Thomas, one of the original partners in the ownership to ask, "Is this the team I have invested a million dollars in?" was on the way to stardom.

In six seasons the DOLPHINS grew from a ragtag expansion team to become a contender for the top honor in the football world.

The city of Miami and all of South Florida was ablaze with pride. Their team was in the Super Bowl. No longer was Miami a sleepy little haven for vacation bound Northerners or a place to retire out of the main stream. Outsiders noticed that the business community was energized with ambition. Commerce and industry began to stir in action as it found its way into the economic life of South Florida.

Five of the 1971 DOLPHINS team members were voted onto the Associated Press All-PRO TEAM. Bob Griese, for his outstanding passing game; Paul Warfield, the man who caught many of those passes; Larry Little; for blocking; Larry Czonka, running and Garo for kicking. This individual achievement was even more remarkable considering that no DOLPHINS had been named to the All-PRO TEAM before that year.

Larry Little is one of the most popular offensive linemen ever to play pro football in Miami. He attended Miami's Booker T. Washington High School. He credits Don Shula for motivating him to success. When Don first came on the scene in Miami Larry weighed 285-pounds. Shula told him he had to lose 20-pounds. Larry toiled in the debilitating summer heat and humidity. He passed out once or twice from dehydration and had to be taken to the clubhouse in a station wagon. His teammates kidded him and said the station wagon was not strong enough to carry him. Larry made his weight limit and his foot speed went up dramatically. He was fast enough to lead the powerful running sweeps of Czonka and Kiick.

Garo says, "Larry was a real demon on the field. His piercing eyes could strike fear into an opposing player's heart. Off the field he was one of the gentlest men you'd ever want to meet. I really appreciated having him in front of me when the opposition would have liked nothing better than to tear my leg off."

Garo's words are a heartfelt tribute to the big man from the little man on the team.

Larry Little was inducted into the Football Hall of Fame in 1993 along with Walter Payton of the Chicago BEARS; Quarterback Dan Fouts, from the San Diego CHARGERS; Bill Walsh, who coached the San Francisco 49'ERS and Chuck Noll, the man who coached the Pittsburgh STEELERS in their Super Bowl years.

The sports writers and sportscasters had a field day

talking about Garo's background and the improbable way he had found his way into the ranks of Pro Football.

Howard Cosell expounded on "the tiemaker-tie breaker theme." When Howard bestowed stardom on a player his booming television voice was heard throughout the land.

Recognition came in from many directions. Garo won the first annual Golden Toe Award from the Thom McAn Shoe Company and Pro Football Weekly. It included a silver trophy and one-thousand dollars in cash. The Benrus Watch Company gave him the Benrus Award.

The Lifesaver Candy Company presented him with its Lifesaver Award for the longest game performance. The Lifesaver Award is presented to an athlete from among all of the professional sports. Tennis star Chris Everts won the award the previous year. The award included a lot of candy from the Lifesaver Company along with a top-of-the-line stereo system.

Garo says, "The most important award for me is that I am finally being recognized as an Armenian. Before this they called me a Greek, or a Greek from Cyprus. There is nothing wrong with being Greek. But, my family background makes me proud and I'm happy to see my Armenian heritage being recognized."

In Armenian communities around the country people were proud to say "I'm Armenian, just like Garo Yepremian."

A writer did a piece in which he wrote about Garo not being selected for the Pro-Bowl and how the "worm turned" in the longest game. Maritza read the article and began to call Garo "Bojeeg." Literally translated from Armenian to English it means worm. Maritza inflection made it a pet name equivalent to someone calling a loved one "my little kitten", "my puppy" etc. It brought a smile to Garo's face.

Now it was time to go to New Orleans for the Super Bowl. The game was to be played in Tulane Stadium at Tulane University. The New Orleans Superdome had not been built at that time.

Super Bowl time in the National Football League is a media circus. The players receive an unusual amount of attention. They are wined and dined by business people and are invited to a continuous round of parties.

Alex Karras the Detroit LIONS lineman was on a newspaper assignment in New Orleans. Alex criticized everything. He didn't like the city and wondered why in the world the NFL would take the Super Bowl game there. Alex complained about the tight-lipped players who didn't want to say anything derogatory about the game conditions. They were all happy to be in the game.

Earlier, Alex made a lot of noise by complaining about the kickers in the league and about Garo Yepremian in particular.

He said, "Garo stands safely on the sidelines and every once in a while he comes in and makes a kick. He runs around yelling 'I keek a touchdown'."

In many of his interviews Garo managed to get in his shots at Alex Karras. Alex was a popular figure with the media and Garo was smart enough to seize the opportunity to do verbal sparring with him.

Garo says, "In truth, Alex and I have a lot of

admiration for each other. When Alex was on the Tonight Show with Johnny Carson he and Johnny got into a discussion about who was the funniest man in the NFL. Alex immediately said 'Garo Yepremian.' I appreciate that kind of publicity."

Garo's good friend Miami sportscaster Bob Sheridan was in New Orleans. He and Garo spent time sightseeing in the city. One night they went to Bourbon Street in the French Quarter. They walked into a bar and saw a show by female impersonators. Garo didn't realize that the performers were men. Bob Sheridan was a little more sophisticated and knew what was going on.

Bob said, "Garo, look at that beautiful woman. She's the prettiest thing I've ever seen. I'm in love. I'm in love."

He reminded Garo of a lovesick rooster crowing to attract the hens.

Near the end of the show Bob told Garo the real sex of the performers and Garo couldn't believe it. He laughed all the way back to the hotel. Of course, when Garo retold the story to his teammates he embellished it so much that every time the players saw Bob they would sing, "I'm in love, I'm in love." It was all part of the fun on-the-road.

Bob Sheridan has been a good friend to Maritza and Garo through the years. Bob eventually left Miami radio and became a champion rodeo bull rider. He is now in the banking business in Boston and is known as Colonel Bob Sheridan. He never lost his love for the media spotlight. Bob is also the ring announcer for Don King's Boxing shows.

By Wednesday of game week Don Shula pulled his

team together and said, "We're all glad we're here and so are the Dallas Cowboys. Tom Landry and Roger Staubach and company didn't come here to lose. They are well prepared. We'd better get serious."

On game day the weather was cold. It was a wet cold and very bothersome to the Miami players. Along with the strong wind it felt like a five degree chill. Krikor was there with some of Garo's friends from Miami. They were wrapped in blankets for the game.

The DOLPHINS turned out to be as cold as the weather.

They lost the game 21-3. The COWBOYS were the team of the day.

In the DOLPHINS locker room after the game the team joined together in a prayer of thanksgiving for everything they had received.

After the prayer Don Shula said, "We've had a wonderful season. We played our best. We don't have to hang our heads. We have to work harder next year so we won't have this disappointment again. I want you to go home, relax and get ready for next year. If each person improves just a little bit we will go all the way. I want to thank you all for what you have done for the team."

This was Don's second loss in a Super Bowl game. He didn't yell or complain about bad breaks or anything he had the right inspirational words at the right time. He is a super sports gentleman in defeat or in victory.

That Super Bowl game was viewed by 23,980,000 viewers on NBC-TV. Professional football and television were a natural match. That was the largest audience ever to watch a one-day event on television.

The next day the DOLPHINS returned to the Miami airport. This time the security people were ready. They set up a podium for the players and had better crowd control.

Garo said, "Even though we lost there was a large crowd of fans there to meet us although they were more subdued than when we returned from the longest game".

The following season of 1972 would make an indelible imprint on Garo's football career.

above... **Trafalgar Square, London, 1961**
   L to R: Garo, Garabed Shirinian, Mom and Dad,
   Krikor, Berj *(front)*

below left... **London, 1962, Garo in soccer uniform**

below right... **1968, Private 1st Class Yepremian,**
   Ft. Leonard, Wood, MO

left... **Garo, the Tiemaker**

below...
**(sons) Garo, Jr., & Azad, Maritza, Garo –
family at play**
(photo, courtesy of Bill Cramer Photography, Philadelphia, PA)

above... **Garo, Jr. and Dad practice**
below... **Azad and Dad practice**
(both photos, courtesy of Bill Cramer Photography, Philadelphia, PA)

above...
**Maritza and Garo
at home**
*(photo, courtesy of
Bill Cramer Photography,
Philadelphia, PA)*

left...
**Krikor (Garo's brother)
and Garo sampling
chocolate**
*(photo, courtesy of
Bill Cramer Photography,
Philadelphia, PA)*

Chapter 13 ?

In the off-season Garo did a variety show on WFUN radio in Miami. It was not strictly a sports program but one in which Garo talked about anything that seemed appropriate. Garo liked to sing. He often imitated Ray Charles and Louis Armstrong. He called it Armenian Soul. His teammates said he was an "unsung" hero. It was fun and the fans loved it.

Garo and Maritza were invited to be the guests of Joe Robbie at the Bath Club for St. Vincent's Ball. That was the most exclusive Catholic social event of the season. Garo was the celebrity guest of the evening. On the society page of the Miami Herald he was described as wearing a velvet tuxedo with satin lapels, blue ruffled shirt and a wide black bow tie. That was a tie that he didn't make. Maritza wore a white V-neck gown with a glittering belt of turquoise and gold-colored stones.

Maritza said to the social reporter, "I got it for my engagement party last year."

Garo added, "Oh yeah, it was a five and dime special."

They did make a charming couple in their picture published in the Herald.

In the playoff game, the championship game and the Super Bowl Garo had made approximately nine-thousand dollars extra for the year. He decided that he would take Maritza on a tour to see his relatives in Soviet Armenia. The trip would take thirty-one days.

To cover his radio program he made thirty-one tapes that would be played while he was away.

They flew to New York and boarded a 747 to Paris. Maritza had never been out of the country. She enjoyed three days of sightseeing in Paris. They visited the Arch De Triumph and the Eiffel Tower. From Paris they went to Poland and on to Moscow.

The cold war was in progress and Garo had to get permission from the National Guard to go into Russia. To go anywhere in the Soviet Union the Russians forced tourists go to Moscow to stay three nights before continuing on their journey. Tourist money was important to the Russians and they wanted the visitors to have ample time to spend it in Moscow. Garo and Maritza had to pre-pay for the entire trip at the Russian Embassy in Washington in order to get a visa. In Moscow a driver and tour guide was assigned to stay with them. The Intourist guide was charged to watch the visitors at all times. The Russians were paranoid about spies.

They checked into the Hotel Leningratska. It was named for Lenin and was a very old hotel that was built in the time of the Czars. Garo and Maritza were escorted to a rickety elevator and taken to the third floor.

Garo says, "When we got to the third floor there was a very tough looking lady sitting behind a table. She had the key to our room. The key was chained to a large piece of rock to prevent loss or theft. The room was equipped with two narrow twin beds and a radio that could only get the government radio station. I knew the Russians were very nosy and the first thing I did was to look for electronic bugs in the room. We were careful what we said. I didn't trust the eavesdroppers."

After some time Garo whispered to Maritza, "Let's sneak out and go to an Armenian restaurant."

They saw some restaurant signs on the way from the airport. They slipped out the back door and tried to hail a cab. After a considerable time a private citizen stopped and took them to an Armenian restaurant. When they walked into the restaurant they could hear music and Armenian songs. Garo was pretty easy to notice. He was wearing a bright red jacket. They were taken to a table that was already occupied. In Moscow there is not much privacy especially in a public restaurant.

The waiter finally came over to them.

Garo said, "We would like to have some shish kabob."

The waiter said, "We don't have any Armenian dishes."

Garo replied, "What do you have. Whatever it is bring it."

The waiter came back with some borscht. It really was just cabbage soup.

Garo got furious and started yelling, "I am an American citizen and I want food. Bring me some food."

Maritza was very nervous about the situation. Garo regained his calm and assured Maritza that they would be all right.

After a time the waiter returned with a large tray of food. There was enough to feed ten people. There was shish kabob on both sides and lots of hamburger. There was so much food that it made Garo feel guilty. He asked an Arab couple at the table to eat some of the food.

Garo says, "They looked at each other and refused to accept the food. They were afraid that they might be accused of collaboration. People in the United States just don't know what it means to be part of an oppressed nation."

They finished eating. Garo and Maritza paid their bill and walked out into a rainy night. They didn't know how to get back to the hotel. Finally they were able to get a cab to stop. The cab was a wreck. One of the windshield wiper blades was missing and the arm was rubbing the glass as it went back and forth. The cab driver stopped and picked up another passenger. He was a drunken Russian soldier. The soldier was loud and obnoxious. The cab arrived at the soldier's destination first. The cab driver and the soldier were arguing about the fare and got into a fistfight. The soldier finally ran away and didn't pay his bill. It was 2:30 A.M. when Garo and Maritza sneaked back into the hotel Leningratska.

The next day they again left the hotel unescorted. The Intourist guide was not doing a good job of keeping them in tow. Perhaps Garo and Maritza were being watched more than they suspected.

On their second day in Moscow they went to the Kremlin and spent the day sightseeing.

On the third morning they packed their suitcases and went downstairs where their guide and driver were waiting. On the way to the airport the guide was dropped off and they proceeded to the airport. The driver said that he had been Lenin's driver during the war. He wanted to give Garo some money so that he could buy American cigarettes. The cigarettes were only sold to tourists. Garo refused to take the driver's money. Instead he used his own money to buy the cigarettes and gave them to the driver. The driver offered him a million thanks he was so glad to get some good American cigarettes.

When they arrived at the airport the driver helped them get seated on the plane. It was a thirty-seat twin-prop Aeroflot plane. Garo and Maritza were seated on the left side. Other people were getting on the plane and talking in Armenian. They didn't know that Garo understood them. The people were complaining because Garo took seats. The plane was overloaded to the point where two people had to sit on crates in the aisle. The plane took off in the cold April weather. The airline people had forgotten to put food on the plane for the four-and-a-half hour flight to Yerevan, Armenia. All they had was water that was served in cardboard cups and pieces of candy that the flight attendant passed out to each passenger. Garo and Maritza had razor blades, hosiery and chewing gum among the items in their bags. Garo got up and began passing out chewing gum. Some of the people took it and some didn't. After Garo shared the chewing gum people opened their bags and shared some oranges with Garo and Maritza. By this time the passengers realized that Garo was an American. Some of the people wanted him to sponsor their sons or daughters so that they could come to the United States to get out of their Iron Curtain misery. Garo couldn't accommodate them because he had to worry about his own cousins who were in the same situation. The people were not allowed to send letters out of Russia. They wanted Garo to take letters out for them. He did take some of the letters. The plane was going over the mountains and the air was really rough. Maritza said a few prayers for their safety. Finally, the plane landed in Yerevan, Armenia where they were weighed as part of the entry procedure. Smugglers would come from Beirut with gold and trade it for diamonds to take out of the country as contraband. The officials counted Garo and Maritza's money. They had to exchange it at the government office and obtain a receipt for the transaction. Upon leaving the country the receipts and money had to match. This was done to prevent them from exchanging the money on the black market.

Garo says, "When they asked to see my money I opened my wallet and showed them that we had about three-thousand dollars in American money. My heart was beating fast. I'm sure my blood pressure went up quite a few points. What they didn't know was that there were ten one-hundred dollar bills hidden away in the walls of the wallet. I was so open about showing them my money that they didn't bother to look for anything more. The three thousand was much more than the average tourist would have had to spend."

Garo and Maritza were cleared through the government office and again assigned to an Intourist guide who took them to the Armenian Hotel in the Center Square of Yerevan, the capital of Armenia. When they arrived at the hotel and entered the lobby there were some drunken soldiers standing around. One of them made a smart remark about Maritza. Garo leaped at him and stuck his finger in his face and told him where to go. The soldier started to fight and the government people stepped in and took him away.

The hotel was terrible. There were two cots in the room and a radio that was full of static. The hotel had fallen into terrible condition under the Soviet regime.

The next day they moved to another hotel named the Ani Hotel. It was a much better place, fairly modern with nice rooms that were comfortable.

Garo was supposed to meet his aunt and a first cousin whom he hadn't seen in twelve years. They lived forty-five miles out of Yerevan. When Garo talked to them on the telephone they told him that government regulations would not let them come to the hotel. They would meet in the public square the next day. When his relatives arrived at the square Garo recognized them from far away and they recognized him. It was a wonderful reunion.

Garo gave them the hosiery, razor blades and finger nail polish that he and Maritza carried over from the United States. The relatives were amazed when he took out the ten one-hundred dollar bills and gave the money to them. They could exchange the American money on the black market for 60 rubles for one American dollar. The government exchange rate was six rubles for one dollar. The relatives thought Garo was a very rich man. In spite of being cut off from news of the world his relatives knew that he was an American football player. They had heard that there was an Armenian kicker playing in the United States. When they heard the name they knew it was Garo.

Maritza had a delightful surprise in Yerevan. Her best friend Adrienne DerOhanessian who grew up with her in Philadelphia was in Yerevan for a year of study. Adrienne was starved for news from home and Maritza was so happy to see a familiar face from Philadelphia.

On the day that they were scheduled to leave Yerevan Garo and Maritza had trouble making plane reservations. They spent most of the day in the travel office. The planned itinerary was tight.

The relatives said, "We'll pick you up at 5:30 tomorrow morning."

At 5:30 the next morning they headed for the airport. There was no place to get food at that time of day and they were very hungry. The flight was to leave at 8:00am. The airport officials announced that there would be a delay because of engine trouble. So it was wait, wait, wait.

Some of the people waiting to board the plane had packed a lot of Armenian cheese and brandy. They started eating and drinking brandy. After a time it was obvious that the group was divided into two political factions. They were drunk and getting angry with each other. One guy who was obnoxiously drunk tried to start a fight with Garo.

At 11:00am the announcement was made that the plane was ready.

Garo's relatives stood behind the wire fence to bid

Maritza and he one final fond farewell. The passengers walked out of the building and were put on two cattle trucks guarded by soldiers. The trucks went about a hundred yards and came to a halt.

The guards said, "We have to go back."

The trucks turned around and they had to spend another hour in the airport. They re-boarded the trucks and were taken out to a huge Russian jet plane. The passengers got on the plane. It was only about half full. At the travel office they had said that there were no seats available. Communications between the airline and the travel office must have been less than adequate.

When the drunken passengers got on the plane Mr. Obnoxious was seated in the back of the plane. He was shouting obscenities. After the plane took off about thirty minutes into the flight when they were over Turkey Mr. Obnoxious got worse.

He said, "I have a knife. I have the power. I'm going to hijack this plane."

He ran to the forward cabin and began beating on the door and tried to open it. He couldn't open the door.

In a minute or two the door opened and a tall man stepped out and said a few words to Mr. Obnoxious. Obnoxious turned and came back and sat five rows ahead of Garo and Maritza on the left side. He didn't make a move after that.

Garo doesn't know what the man said to Obnoxious. His talk must have contained a reference to Siberia or some other terrible place that no one wanted to go. It certainly quieted him and kept peace on the plane.

They landed in Beirut, Lebanon and went through

customs. They called a porter who took their baggage and put it on a handcart. On the way through the airport the porter cut in front of another cart. A police officer ran over and punched the porter right in the face. Those people were tough on each other. All of the shenanigans and hooliganism on the trip made Maritza extremely nervous. Outside the airport they got a cab and went to the Phonicia Hotel on the waterfront. After checking in they went out and got a cab and asked the driver to take them to an Armenian hotel.

The cab driver was Armenian he said, "I know a good place for you. The cook makes shiskabob over real charcoal and he has other good Armenian food."

They had a wonderful meal. After dinner they walked by the seaside where they saw an American Corvair automobile burning on the beach. Maritza bought some green almonds from a yelling street vendor. When they got back to the Phonicia Hotel they estimated that they had walked three or four miles. Maritza ate green almonds during the walk and they made her sick.

They stayed a couple of days in Beirut and visited the Gold Market. The Gold Market is a narrow street about a mile long. Both sides of the street are lined with jewelry stores. A small shop about three by eight feet in area is likely to have many thousands of dollars worth of gold jewelry on display. At one shop an old man was seated at a bench making a piece of gold jewelry. Maritza spotted a bracelet made of 24-carat gold with gold coins attached to it.

Before they arrived at the gold market Garo told Maritza that they would only speak in English when they talked to the shopkeepers.

Garo said, "How much is this bracelet?"

The man answered, "One-thousand American dollars."

Garo, "That is too much. I can only pay three-hundred dollars."

The old man turned and spoke to his brother using a combination of Greek and Turkish words which Garo understood very well.

The man said to his brother, "How much do we have invested in this piece?"

Brother answered, "We have about three-hundred dollars in that one."

The older man said to Garo, "We must get at least five-hundred dollars to make just a little bit of profit."

Garo and the gold merchant kept haggling over the price. All the while Garo had the advantage because he could understand their private conversation that they thought was in a language he didn't know.

The final price was three-hundred-sixty dollars.

The shopkeeper said, "For your beautiful lady and because you are someone we would like to have as a good friend we will let you have this beautiful piece of jewelry. Perhaps you will come back to our humble shop and do some more business with us."

The people in the Gold Market love the back and forth negotiations that go with every deal. They always ask a lot more than what they expect to receive.

And by the way, they didn't visit the street where Garo had guided the Greek and Turkish men on his way from Larnaca to London in 1960.

After a few days they flew out of Beirut and landed at the only airport on Cyprus at Nicosia. They were greeted by a gang of Garo's relatives. His relatives were very familiar with his fame as a kicker for the Miami DOLPHINS. They all thought that he was a millionaire for sure. His relatives insisted that Garo and Maritza stay at their house in Nicosia. Garo wanted to go to a hotel because he knew that he would have more privacy there. The relatives finally prevailed and Garo agreed to stay at their house.

Garo's uncle Robert drove them to see the old neighborhoods in Larnaca and Lefka, Cyprus.

They journeyed back to the house where Garo lived as a child. There was the balcony where young Garo peed down over old Gamovour's candy. Maritza laughed when Garo told her the story.

Garo felt very emotional when he looked at the old church wall where he had spent so much time kicking his soccer ball.

He says, "The cement stucco had broken off in many places and had been patched with new cement. I wanted to go over and put my arms on the wall and maybe even kiss it. I couldn't forget the time in 1966 in Minnesota when I was almost frightened out of my mind about kicking in the National Football League. My vivid memory of the ants and grasshoppers on the wall helped me clear my brain of all fear of the game. It allowed me to set a new record for the number of field goals in a single game. Many other times in my career that wall helped me get through some tense moments. That wall means a lot to me."

"The Armenian school and the American Academy seemed a lot smaller than they did when I was a kid. As we grow older and travel things in our childhood don't seem as important as they once did. Maybe that's why people say you can't go home again."

After seven days he found that he was eager to leave and get on with the trip.

They left Cyprus and flew to London and stayed at the London Hilton.

On the way from the airport to the hotel Maritza started crying in the back seat of the cab. She had a bad case of homesickness. This was the first time she had been out of the United States and the whole business of the trip was wearing on her. She wanted Garo to have a good time. She pulled herself together and tried to keep a happy face. They could see the Queen's Gardens from the balcony of their hotel.

Garo said to Maritza, "When I was a fabric cutter in London I would dream about having lunch or a drink at the Hilton. I never thought that I could stay here. It was a foolish dream. I might as well have dreamed that I would become King of England. But honey, here we are."

They visited Garo's Uncle Jack in London. One night Uncle Jack was driving them back to the hotel when a man leaped in front of the car. He slid up the hood and broke the windshield. It was unnerving to say the least. The man crawled off of Jack's car and said he was unhurt. He walked away. Jack drove carefully the rest of the way to the hotel.

They left London and returned to their home in Florida. They felt like they were back in the promised land.

Late in May Garo was scheduled to go for his National Guard duty at Camp Blanding. He was interviewed by a newspaper reporter about the rigors and routine upsetting due to military service.

Garo responded, "You know just being away for a

few weeks on that trip made me want to hurry and get back here. I showed Maritza some fairly well off people from my country and what their living conditions would be called here-ghetto. You can't compare it. I just wanted her to thank God for what we have. Everyone should spend a couple of weeks away from this country so that they would realize what great opportunities and freedoms they have here. Then they wouldn't complain. They'd be very, very, happy if they only knew. I remember what happened to my grandfather and grandmother under oppression and tyranny and then I know that a little military service is a small price to pay for the opportunity to live in freedom in the United States."

The taproot of his soul was now firmly implanted in the U.S.A.

Chapter 14 ?

1972 was destined to be one of the most important years in Garo's drive to be the number one kicker in the NFL. Krikor was transferred to Florida by the Ford Motor Company. His job required that he travel a lot. He had to drive to Jacksonville at least two times a week to work with the dealerships there.

One day Krikor told Garo that he had fallen asleep at the wheel on the way back from Jacksonville and was lucky not to have had a wreck.

Garo said, "You don't need that job. Why don't you take over the necktie business, here."

Krikor set up the main office in North Miami. He opened the first store in the Cutler Ridge Mall followed by stores in Fort Lauderdale and in the Midway Mall in Miami. He also sold some franchises on the West Coast.

People are intrigued with a story whereby an unlikely person suddenly becomes famous. We all dream our impossible dreams and many times reality seems as distant as the stars. The idea that a person who makes and sells neckties could make it big shows us that maybe our dreams aren't so impossible after all. The radio, TV and newspaper people knew that this was a "grabber" of a story and they played it for all it was worth. Garo, the "tiemaker-tiebreaker" was a media star.

Behind the facade of tiemaker-tiebreaker Garo was working hard to stay in condition and live up to Don Shula's expectation that each player would come to camp in 1972 just a little bit better than he was after the Super Bowl loss in New Orleans. Garo jogged everyday. When the weather was bad he would take the car out of the garage and use the garage as an indoor running track. He'd go twenty-five laps in one direction and then switch and run twenty-five laps in the other direction. In the confines of his garage he didn't want to work the muscles on one side more than the other.

Garo's father and mother sold their house in Detroit and made plans to come to live in Miami. Sarkis stayed in Detroit to take care of the house settlement and Azadouhi and Sarko went to Cyprus for a month so that Sarko could be in touch with his relatives in the old country. Sarkis settled his real estate deal and moved to Miami to live with Garo and Maritza. He planned to buy a house in Miami. After searching the area they found a home on a private lake. From the living room it had a beautiful view of the swimming pool in the backyard and the lake beyond. Azadouhi always talked about having a home with a beautiful view.

Before the start of the 1972 football season Azadouhi and Sarko arrived at the Miami airport from their trip to Cyprus. Garo and his family members met them at the airport. On the drive home Sarkis told Azadouhi about the new house.

Garo chimed in and said, "Mom, the house is nice but you have to remember we can't afford a real mansion. This house may not be what you want. Don't be disappointed, it will do nicely until we can afford something you really want."

He was deliberately downplaying the qualities of the home. Krikor added his words of caution to the conversation.

When they drove into the driveway Azadouhi thought, "Oooh, this is a nice neighborhood."

She walked into the living room and saw the beautiful scene through the window. Overcome with emotion she cried. Through tears of joy she said, "This is the home of my dreams. No, no, I never dreamed I could live in a home this nice. Is it really ours?"

Tears streamed down Garo's cheeks.

Garo said, "It makes me so happy to see Mom happy."

His Mom was a pillar of strength for the entire family.

During the dark days when he was dropped by the Detroit LIONS it was she who cut and sewed the neckties that were sold to help them eke out a living. Garo loves to tell the stories about the time his Mom fought with Old Gamovour when he ruined Gamovour's candy birds beneath the balcony in Larnaca, Cyprus; Mom who told the Priest from the church that she would scrub the walls of the churchyard; Mom who took him out of the Armenian school and enrolled me in the American Academy; and a thousand other things that only Moms can do.

Miami opened the 1972 season against the Kansas City Chiefs on September 17th. The sun beat down on the field with mid-summer intensity. The temperature on the artificial surface of newly opened Arrowhead Stadium was estimated at 120 degrees Fahrenheit. Don Shula said his team works best when it is real hot.

At the end of the 3rd quarter when most of the CHIEFS players were dragging themselves from one end of the field to the other 265-pound DOLPHINS guard Larry Little sprinted to his side of the field. It was demoralizing. That whole episode told the CHIEFS that the DOLPHINS were in better physical condition than they.

The DOLPHINS controlled the game on the ground. Mercury Morris gained sixty-seven yards on fourteen rushes. He caught a pass for seven yards and ran a kickoff back for thirty-three yards. Mercury was from West Texas State and was in his fourth season. The scoring started in the first quarter when Quarterback Bob Griese completed a pass to Marlin Briscoe. Garo scored on a 47-yard field goal in the first half. The DOLPHINS led 17-0 at the half. Garo followed with another in the second half. The final score was DOLPHINS 20-CHIEFS 10. It was the first opening game victory for Don Shula as the DOLPHINS coach.

On the following Sunday the DOLPHINS beat the Houston OILERS 34 to 13. The Miami ground game was awesome. Jim Kiick, Larry Czonka and Mercury Morris were too much for the OILERS on that day. Garo missed an extra point after the second DOLPHINS touchdown. It was a rare occasion when he missed a point after.

The third game of the season was played in Minnesota against the VIKINGS and their Purple People Eater defense. The DOLPHINS were trailing 14-6 late in the fourth quarter. Garo was sent in to go for a field goal from fifty-one yards out. The kick was good and that made it 14-9. The 51-yard field goal was a personal record for Garo. The DOLPHINS regained possession after the ensuing kickoff and moved the ball down the field with very little time left. Bob Griese threw a pass to Jim Mandich for the game winning touchdown. Garo's extra point put Miami in the lead 16-14.

He was voted the winner of the Golden Toe Award for the week. Garo's long field goal and that last second touchdown pass were two of several small miracles that contributed to the DOLPHINS unbeaten season.

The DOLPHINS No Name Defense showed its mettle in the season's fourth game against the New York JETS. Joe Namath and his team was a force to be reckoned with. The No Name Defense stood its ground and stopped the JETS on the goal line when they were first and ten on the one yard line late in the third quarter. The final score was Miami 27-New York 17.

There they were with four wins and no losses and leading the American conference.

Don Shula said, "The start of our schedule has to be as tough as anybody started out with. Those four were dynamite."

Adversity appeared on the DOLPHINS schedule in game five against the San Diego CHARGERS. On October 15th on the fourteenth play in the first quarter Miami Quarterback Bob Griese faded back to throw a pass. Deacon Jones and Ron East broke through the DOLPHINS offensive line. Griese threw the ball. It left his hand at the instant Jones and East slammed into him. The DOLPHINS quarterback was lying on the turf in great pain.

"The first thing I knew," says Griese, "I was under somebody and my ankle was hurting. I didn't have to see the stretcher to know that I was going out."

Bob Griese had a broken bone in his leg and a badly dislocated ankle. On the sidelines, Garo and the entire defensive unit looked on in horror. Their chances of a return match in the Super Bowl dimmed as hope flittered away.

The season seemed to be slipping away. The stage was set for one of the all time greatest "coming off the bench" relief roles in all of professional football. Earl Morral, a 38-year-old crew cut veteran, had been picked up on waivers from the Baltimore COLTS. For sixteen years he played a backup role for Detroit, Pittsburgh, the New York GIANTS, and Baltimore. Now the DOLPHINS needed him.

The first time the DOLPHINS got the ball after Griese's injury Morral worked the ball into field goal range. Garo went in and scored with a 37-yard kick. Every player on the offensive and defensive units along with the special team players rose to magnificence. Earl Morral called plays and passes to perfection. His brilliant relief job let the DOLPHINS survive the shocking loss of their quarterback. Miami defeated the San Diego Chargers 24-10.

Reflecting on Game six against the Buffalo BILLS middle linebacker Nick Buoniconti said, "It was the most ridiculous game I've ever participated in. If I never play in another one like it I'll be the happiest guy in the world."

Outside linebacker Doug Swift said, "The only weirder game I can remember was back in high school. Every time the officials got a chance they dropped a flag."

At half time the Buffalo BILLS were leading the DOLPHINS 13-7.

Defensive tackle Manny Fernandez was in the hospital with pneumonia two days before the game. He hung tough and suited up for the game. In his weakened condition he played the entire game. Manny wears thick glasses off the field.

He says, "Without my glasses I can just make out the number of the guy playing next to me. I can't see the scoreboard. I'm legally blind."

On the second play of the second half Fernandez changed the game. In spite of feeling weak and having blurred vision he sensed that the next play by Buffalo would be a pass. He went one-on-one with the offensive guard. Manny charged into the opposing backfield. The play turned out to be a draw play and when the Buffalo quarterback wanted to give the ball to the BILLS O.J. Simpson, Manny Fernandez was there to take the hand off. He ran it back to the BILLS ten yard line and Czonka took it in on the next play for a touchdown. Garo made the extra point and the DOLPHINS led 14-13. The next time the DOLPHINS got the ball Garo booted a 54-yard field goal. It was the longest field goal of his career up to that time. Garo and his teammates were equal to the challenge. The final score was Miami 24-Buffalo 23.

Game six of the 1972 season was a perfect example

of Don Shula's coaching philosophy-never give up and always take advantage of the breaks when they come.

After game six some of the players began to worry about the necessity of losing a game. They reasoned that it was impossible to go through an entire season unbeaten and that fate might deal them a losing hand in the playoffs. The semi-final playoffs followed by the league championship game and the big one, the Super Bowl were like a sudden death second season for the teams in the NFL.

Game seven in Baltimore presented an emotional problem for Earl Morral. He played for four years with the Baltimore COLTS as backup quarterback to Johnny Unitas. He had many friends on the Baltimore team. Morral and Unitas exchanged pleasantries at the midfield coin toss and then it was on to the business of professional football. Garo had special memories in Baltimore. He had come a long way in his career since the day he kicked off for the Detroit LIONS and ran off to sit on the wrong bench. He was an integral part of the super football team that brought fame to Miami. The game was a shutout. The No Name Defense did a perfect job.

Don Shula said, "Special team players are special people. It takes a special knack. You have to be reckless in an intelligent way. If you don't have the heart you can't get the job done."

He said that in tribute to the heroics of Curtis Johnson and Lloyd Mumphord. Curtis was a three-year veteran who was a first string cornerback and who did double duty on the special teams. In the second quarter he broke through on a Baltimore punt attempt and blocked the kick. The ball was recovered by the

DOLPHINS on the COLTS 25-yard line. The offensive team scored for Miami and the score was 13-0. Garo went in for the extra point. The kick was blocked and the score remained 13-0. Lloyd Mumphord was used as a fifth defensive back in passing situations and served extra duty on special teams for the DOLPHINS. In the second quarter Lloyd Mumphord knocked down a 54-yard field goal attempt by Boris Shlapak. The DOLPHINS got the ball and drove to the 24-yard line. Garo laid up a field goal to make the score 16-0 at halftime. They scored another touchdown in the second half. Garo's extra point made it 23-0. That was the final score.

The No Name Defense was justifiably proud.

"Holding your opponent scoreless is something every defensive team tries to do," said linebacker Mike Kolen. "That's our job and when you see a big zero on the board you know you did your job."

It was a fine achievement at the halfway point of the 1972 season.

After beating the Buffalo BILLS 30-16 O.J. Simpson said, "It's going to be tough for them to get beat. I think they're the best team in football."

During the training film sessions on practice days Shula would re-run certain plays that displeased him in the previous Sunday's game. Over and over the films would play with Shula and his coaches criticizing the players moves and offering remedial suggestions.

There was so much attention placed on the bad plays in the Buffalo game that linebacker Doug Swift asked, "Coach did we win that game?"

In one of the film sessions when the coaching critique was concentrated on the actions of the special teams the offensive linemen were seated in the rear of the room. Boredom was their biggest problem. Offensive guard Larry Little passed gas. That started a contest to see which one could fart the loudest.

Don Shula became angry at the disruption and inattention. He thought each player should be interested in every move made in a game. It was part of his coaching philosophy.

He yelled, "Close the doors and enjoy. We're leaving. Offensive linemen stay here. Coaches out!. We're getting out of this juvenile stinkhole."

Offensive line coach John Sandusky had been a coach under Shula in Baltimore and made the switch to Miami with Shula in 1970. John remained loyal to his linemen and refused to leave the room with the rest of the team.

Later John said, "It takes more than a few farts to break our loyalty to each other on this line."

Hannibal crossed the Alps.

Columbus discovered America.

Washington crossed the Delaware.

On November 12th, 1972, Don Shula reached one-hundred victories in ten years of coaching. The DOLPHINS whipped the PATRIOTS 52-0.

Don Shula enrolled in John Carroll University in Cleveland in 1947. Father Birkenbaur was also a newcomer to the University. He was assigned to teach trigonometry. He remembers Don as a bright young student who had the respect of other people. Father Birkenbaur says respect is an important part of leadership.

On November 13th, President Richard Nixon sent a telegram that said:

"HEARTIEST CONGRATULATIONS ON VICTORY NO. 100. YOU HAVE DONE SOMETHING NO OTHER COACH IN PROFESSIONAL FOOTBALL HAS EVER ACCOMPLISHED-100 VICTORIES IN YOUR FIRST TEN YEARS-AND THE DOLPHINS RECORD THIS YEAR IS NOTHING LESS THAN SENSATIONAL. THIS NEW MILESTONE IS CONVINCING PROOF OF YOUR SUPERIOR COACHING ABILITY AND, THEREFORE, I WILL DO MY VERY BEST TO RESIST SUGGESTING ANY MORE PLAYS SHOULD YOU GO THROUGH THE PLAYOFFS AND ON TO THE SUPER BOWL AGAIN."

President Nixon felt obligated to root for the Washington REDSKINS.

In the game against the PATRIOTS the DOLPHINS set a number of club records:

Most points scored in a game;

A team record 482-yards in total offense;

A club record of only 92-yards allowed rushing;

A club record of two shutouts in one season.

On the following Sunday the DOLPHINS won a bruising game against the New York JETS 28 to 24.

The DOLPHINS continued their heroics with wins against the St. Louis CARDINALS 31-10, the New England PATRIOTS 37-21 and the New York GIANTS 23-13.

Garo contributed a barrage of field goals in those victories.

In spite of the string of victories, Shula and his coaches were critical of all bad plays during the film sessions and in practice. They ran the plays over and over again making comments about who did what and why the play failed.

The offensive line must be good for any football team to have an effective offense. Center Jim Langer, guards Larry Little and Bob Kuchenberg, tackles Norm Evans, Doug Crusan and Wayne Moore, tight ends Marv Fleming and Jim Mandich, they are the men who helped Larry Czonka gain 1,117 yards and Mercury Morris to gain 1,000 yards. The DOLPHINS were the first team in history to have two 1,000 yard gainers in the same season.

Bob Kuchenberg said, "Offensive linemen don't have statistics. The defense has its tackle chart and interceptions and quarterbacks their passing stats, the running backs-you know, everyone else is measured in some way by statistics. But not us. So, we look at that rushing record as a gauge of our efficiency."

One game stood in the way of a perfect regular season for the DOLPHINS. They were to play the Baltimore COLTS on the final day of the season. Garo contributed to that victory with field goals from the 40, 50 and 35-yard lines. The final score was DOLPHINS 16 Colts 0.

There was a very dramatic moment in the final minutes of the fourth quarter of the game against Baltimore. Bob Griese took over for Earl Morral at quarterback. The crowd of 80,000 fans gave a standing ovation to both men. Griese performed well completing two of three passes.

The regular season ended and the "second season" of playoff games began.

In the American Conference semi-final playoff game against the Cleveland BROWNS the DOLPHINS scored first on a punt blocked by Charlie Babb. On their second possession The DOLPHINS moved from their own 16-yard line to the Cleveland 33. One of the big plays was an end around run by Paul Warfield for a 21-yard gain. The drive bogged down and Garo came on to the field and booted a field goal to give the DOLPHINS a 10-0 lead. The BROWNS made their first score midway in the third quarter to trim the lead to 10-7. A little later Garo kicked a 47-yard field goal to extend the lead to 13-7. With just 8:11 left in the game Cleveland quarterback Mike Phipps hit Fair Hooker with a 27-yard touchdown pass. For the first time since game number three the DOLPHINS trailed in the fourth quarter. They faced possible elimination from the post-season action. At 6:49 in the fourth quarter Earl Morral and Paul Warfield teamed up to drive the DOLPHINS from their own twenty to a first down on the Cleveland 20-yard line. Mercury Morris went into the line for a two yard gain followed by an interference call on Cleveland linebacker Bill Andrews against Warfield. The ball was on the BROWNS 8-yard line. On the next play tackle Norm Evans and guard Bob Kuchenberg swept the defending linemen out of the way and Jim Kiick went across for the touchdown. Garo's extra point kick made the score DOLPHINS 20-BROWNS 14. With five minutes remaining in the game the BROWNS weren't out of yet. The BROWNS fought to the DOLPHINS 34-yard marker and the NO Name Defense stiffened. With 1:15 left to play in the game Mike Phipps threw a pass to his tight end Mike Morin. The DOLPHINS Doug Swift stepped in front of the receiver and intercepted the pass. The final score of this hard fought game was 20-14 in favor of the DOLPHINS. Their next test would come when they moved into the Championship game against the Pittsburgh STEELERS, in Pittsburgh.

The STEELERS were the Cinderella team of 1972. They played to the top of the AFC Central Division to win their first title in forty years. When a team went into Pittsburgh they not only played the forty players on the STEELERS team they also played against the hometown crowds. The red, green and white flags of Franco Harris' army, Gerela's Gorillas in Gorilla suits and arm bands on John Fuqua's Legions kept the 52,000 fans in the game.

The Championship game was tied 7-7 at the end of the first half. Early in the third quarter the STEELERS moved ahead 10-7 on a Roy Gerela field goal.

In the third quarter Don Shula asked Bob Griese if he thought he was ready for action.

Griese said, "Yes."

Bob Griese entered the game with 10:50 left in the third quarter. He promptly sent the DOLPHINS downfield on an 80-yard drive for a 14-10 lead. The DOLPHINS won the game 21-17 to make it 16 wins and no defeats for the season. They were going to the SUPER BOWL VII against the Washington RED-SKINS in Los Angeles.

During the week before the SUPER BOWL the intense media attention worried the coaches as they tried to get their teams physically and emotionally ready for the confrontation.

Maritza and her Mom, Azadouhi and brother Krikor flew in during the week and stayed at the Beverly Hills Hilton. The players were housed in Long Beach.

On game day the Apollo 17 astronauts led the

90,182 fans in the pledge of allegiance. The LITTLE
ANGELS CHOIR sang the national anthem and one
thousand pigeons were released to fly over the
stadium. This was definitely a big time sports event.
27,450,000 viewers were watching on television.

The DOLPHINS scored in the first and second
quarters to take a 14-0 lead. The score remained the
same until 2:07 left in the game. Garo trotted out to
attempt a 42-yard field goal that would have made the
score 17-0.

As soon as Shula called for the field goal team
Garo was apprehensive. In the pre-game warmups his
kicks were going low. The two extra points earlier in
the game had barely cleared the cross bar.

Earl Morral said, "Garo, am I tilting the ball wrong
or anything else that bothers you?

"No. I'll be ok."

There wasn't that much pressure on this try. The
DOLPHINS had a comfortable lead late in the game.
However, football game action can turn for the better
or worse on a single play or series of plays. The famous
Heidi game proved that long ago.

The DOLPHINS broke out of the huddle and the
players took their places in the field goal setup.
Howard Kindig bent over to snap the ball and the
offensive line tensed for action. Earl Morral, the
holder, called for the snap. Garo took his measured
steps and his left foot struck the ball. Everything was
very routine up to that point. The ball left Garo's foot
on a low line. What happened next has been discussed
and talked about at sports banquets and on sports talk
shows in the years that followed. In the selective
memories of the people who played in the game or

watched the game the ball must have been in several places at the same time. It has been reported that the football either hit several of the Miami players or was blocked by half of the REDSKINS team.

Bob Heinz played defensive tackle in regular formations for the DOLPHINS. He was switched to the offensive line in field goal kicking situations. Bob says that the kick by Garo hit him in the back of the head and almost took his helmet off. Bill Brundige of the REDSKINS was charging on the play and may have pushed Heinz backwards. Brundige is generally credited with the block of the field goal attempt. The ball bounced back and from that point on the outcome of the game was in doubt. The ball was loose on the turf about three yards to Garo's right. Earl Morral jumped up and made a valiant attempt to stop the onrushing Brundige. He was unable to put him on the ground.

Garo leaped for the ball and tried to make something out of the play. He saw a DOLPHIN jersey out in the right flat. It was most likely Larry Czonka who was supposed to go out for a possible pass on a "busted" field goal play. Garo quickly brought his right arm back. The ball slipped out of his grasp and flew straight up into the air. When the ball came down Garo batted at it in an attempt to knock it out of bounds and end the play. The ball ricocheted into the arms of the REDSKINS' Mike Bass who took it into the DOLPHINS end zone for a REDSKINS touchdown. The score was now 14-7 giving the REDSKINS a chance to tie the game in the remaining time and send it into overtime. The game was shaping up as another remarkable finish in the NFL.

Garo came off the field and sensed the fear and antagonism in the DOLPHINS players.

Don Shula said, "You should have sat on the damn ball."

Garo thought, "Why me? Why me?"

He says, "When you really care about your team, your coaches, family and fans and you make a mistake it seems like you have killed somebody."

Offensive tackle Norm Evans came over and put his arm around Garo and said, "Garo, don't worry about it God loves you and our defense will stop them. And you know what, in all things...give thanks to God. There is a reason for all things."

Garo knew what Norm meant.

Norm's nickname was Pope IV. He had written a book entitled ON GOD's SQUAD. He led the team's chapel service every Sunday morning and was largely responsible for the closeness that existed among the DOLPHIN players.

Norm Evans graduated from Texas Christian University and played for one year with the Houston OILERS and then came to the DOLPHINS in the expansion year 1966. Norm and Howard Twilley are two players who stayed with the team through the bad early years and on into the golden years in the '70's.

Garo says, "The more you are around Norm Evans the greater he becomes. His status does not diminish with familiarity."

In the final minutes of Super Bowl VII Garo, the hero in the previous year's playoffs against the Kansas City CHIEFS was wearing the goat horns solidly on his head.

He thought, "What a shame. The players have

worked like dogs to make it to this point and I have put them all in jeopardy."

Krikor said, "As soon as the kick was blocked I knew Washington was going to score. I sweated like I never sweated before, from top to bottom. I didn't know what to expect. There were a little more than two minutes left in the game and anything could happen."

As Norm Evans predicted the No Name Defense rose to the challenge and held its ground. Bill Standfill and Vern Den Herder sacked the RED-SKINS Billy Kilmer on the last play of the game and the DOLPHINS were the champions of the football world.

In the dressing room Pete Rozelle presented Don Shula with the Vince Lombardi Trophy.

The reporters crowded around Garo's locker space and asked a lot of questions about the pass. Garo was uncharacteristically subdued during the interviews.

He finished by saying, "Thank God we won."

His friend Bob Sheridan came by and said, "Garo, this is good for you. The fans will never forget you."

Garo, "They'll never forgive me."

Krikor said, "Don't worry about it. We're going to celebrate."

Garo, "You people are nuts. How can I forget about it when I know I've had a bad day?"

Garo showered, dressed and joined Maritza and the other family members for the victory dinner at the Beverly Hills Hilton. Garo was quiet during the dinner. He was embarrassed to face his teammates.

After about fifteen minutes he began to get sharp pains on the right side of his body. He begged Krikor to leave with him because he was ready to fall over.

Krikor helped him to the car. Garo had excruciating pain radiating down his right side from his neck to his foot. By sheer will power he was able to walk unassisted out of the dining room and into the hallway. When he was out of sight of his teammates Krikor supported him so he could walk.

They drove to the team hotel in Long Beach. Krikor helped him get to his room where Garo asked for some ice from the ice machine to put in the bath tub. Krikor made several trips to the ice machines. Garo got into the icy bath and soaked for about five minutes. After he got out of the tub and dried himself the pain left never to return again.

Garo says, "It's hard to explain. I know I was in great pain and yet, the ice water bath cured it completely. The pain must have come from nervous tension because of the bad pass."

The team arrived back in Miami. A large crowd milled around at the airport. A special stand was in place and plenty of police were on hand for crowd control.

Don Shula summed it up, "This is the greatest moment in my coaching life. This is the greatest team I've ever been associated with. We've won the big one. This is the ultimate. Seventeen and 0 says it all."

The players came to the microphone to talk about the game. There was a steady chant from the crowd "Garo, Garo, Garo!" Fans were holding up signs that said "Garo, we love you."

They wanted Garo to talk about "the pass."

He said, "I tried to make something out of a bad situation and it backfired. Thank God we won. I promise not to throw a pass again until the next Super Bowl."

Within a week after Super Bowl VII Norm Evans' words spoken to Garo on the sideline after the kick began to come true. Garo was besieged with offers to speak at off-season banquets and meetings. The flip side of a near football tragedy created the most memorable event in his career. His first, last, and only pass took on an identity all of its own. "THE PASS" has kept Garo's name alive and out of the abyss of the forgotten in the turbulent world of football.

Chapter 15 &

The off-season was exciting for Garo. He made comedy out of tragedy.

He said, "President Nixon made me throw the pass. Since I don't have my citizenship papers yet I thought I'd better throw it."

He said, "George Blanda is a quarterback and kicker who makes a lot of money. If I can complete a pass I can ask Joe Robbie for an increase in pay."

A Miami auto dealership started a "Garo for Quarterback" club. They gave a free necktie to each club member.

Privately Garo was thankful that God gave him something that caused the fans to remember him.

Garo was a guest on television with Bob Hope at the Fountainbleau Hotel. Bob asked Garo who his writers were and of course Garo had no writers. He was naturally funny. The DOLPHIN fans said he was the funniest man to come to Miami since Jackie Gleason made it his home.

That off-season marked another milestone in his life. Garo graduated with the class of '73 in Madison County, Indiana. Although he did not need a diploma to be successful in Pro Football he was extremely happy to get that diploma. He was supposed to be in the class of '60 at the American Academy in Larnaca, Cyprus. Two weeks before graduation the civil war between the Greeks and Turks escalated. The Armenians were neutral although they were sympathetic to the Greeks.

Garo says, "Innocent people were getting killed by stray bullets. That's when my family decided to relocate in London."

When Garo tried to enroll at Butler University Gary Nash was a student who did the college radio broadcasts of the football games. Quite naturally he followed Garo's career in the NFL. He knew that Garo never had the opportunity to get his High School diploma. Gary was instrumental in having Garo's transcript sent from Cyprus to Frankton High School and to get it evaluated for an equivalency diploma. In the spring of 1973 Garo accepted a diploma from Frankton at an assembly in the school gym. He told the assembled students and faculty that he considered himself a specialist in human relations. Garo's ability to express his feelings in easy to understand words was a great gift that would help him overcome adversity in later years.

In those off-season speeches Garo made a lot of jokes about being baldheaded.

He said, "I'm much lighter this way. I can run faster. Being bald never bothered me."

Garo grew a long mustache.

"I look like that old time movie actor who had that mustache. What's his name? Gable, yeah, Clark Gable. I've got the same build as him anyway. Maybe I will market my own hair conditioner."

Those were the golden days for the DOLPHINS and Garo was a highly visible member of the team. His days and nights were filled with radio shows, television interviews and banquet appearances.

The 1973 season was a continuation of the '72 unbeaten season.

Linebacker Nick Buoniconti warned, "You can be a champion one year and a bum the next and that's happened to most of the teams that won the Super Bowl."

On the first day of training camp Shula had a field goal kicking drill.

He said, "Garo, we'll throw the ball past you. I want you to turn and fall on the ball."

On the second try Garo fell and twisted his ankle and was laid up for four days. That was the end of that drill.

The DOLPHINS opened the season in the Orange Bowl with a 21-13 victory over the San Francisco 49ERS. The heat reached 100 degrees on the field and 49ERS Quarterback John Brodie had to sit out most of the second half. The heat didn't stop the DOLPHINS. They brought the ball within field goal range four times and Garo connected from 31, 53, 45 and 22 yards. A touchdown and a safety accounted for the other points.

The Oakland RAIDERS broke the DOLPHINS string of victories in the second game of the season. The RAIDERS beat the DOLPHINS 12-7 with John Madden coaching.

The DOLPHINS went on to win the next ten games and then Baltimore beat them 16-3.

When the regular season and preliminary post season games ended the DOLPHINS were in SUPER BOWL VIII against the Minnesota VIKINGS and their Purple People Eater defensive unit.

The game was played on January 13, 1974 in Houston, Texas.

In the days prior to the game the sportscasters and reporters were on their usual hunt for interesting interviews.

In response to questions about Garo's pass in Super Bowl VII Don Shula said, "Garo is forbidden to pass. We've had special equipment made for him."

Garo said, "Yes, Coach Shula has boxing gloves for me in case I want to pick up the ball with my hands. I'm definitely going to wear those boxing gloves in Sunday's game."

Maritza, Krikor and younger brother Berj flew out to Houston for the game. Berj was in high school and this was his first Super Bowl. Krikor was in high spirits. He bought cowboy hats for Berj, Garo and himself. He also purchased some big cigars. He was ready to celebrate.

Maritza had been pregnant and lost her baby with a miscarriage in October. At Super Bowl time she was pregnant again.

With a sold out stadium and 75-million fans watching on television the DOLPHINS scored two touchdowns in the first quarter. Garo followed with a 28-yard field goal in the second quarter. The score was 17-0 at half time. Maritza went to the ladies room at half time. She had some cramps and was worried about another miscarriage. She asked Berj to walk with her to the ladies room. He waited outside and when Maritza came out she wasn't feeling well. Berj was worried as he and Maritza went off to find the first aid area. When they got there the attendants called an ambulance and took Maritza to the hospital in Houston. Her symptoms suggested that she might be on the verge of another miscarriage. Berj rode in the ambulance with Maritza and didn't get to see the last half of the game.

Garo knew where Maritza would be sitting and had patted his helmet to acknowledge her presence in the first half. Maritza knew that Garo would be worried when she was missing in the second half. After the doctor examined her at the hospital he gave her a shot and released her. She didn't have any pain although there was some spotting of her undergarments.

Maritza and Berj intended to get a taxi to take them back to the stadium. They couldn't find a taxi. They were all at the game. Maritza and Berj walked all the way back to the stadium. Maritza was anxious to get back to meet Garo outside the locker room.

In the meantime, Krikor was in the press box where the rumor spread that Maritza was taken to the hospital and that she had lost the baby.

The final score of the game was 24-7.

Garo thought, "This year I didn't do anything wrong. Now we can really celebrate. I don't smoke or drink but I'll wear one of Krikor's cowboy hats and wave one of his big cigars."

Krikor rushed to Garo's side and said, "I'm sorry but Maritza lost the baby."

Garo was crushed. His hopes and dreams of having his own family were broken.

NFL Commissioner Pete Rozelle came into the DOLPHINS locker room for the trophy presentation. He immediately summoned a police car to take Garo and Krikor to the hospital.

The police drove at a high rate of speed with sirens wailing. Garo and Krikor were on the way to the hospital and unbeknown to them Maritza and Berj were walking back to the stadium. They had to fight the traffic and the crowd leaving after the game. When Maritza arrived at the stadium she immediately went to the team bus where the DOLPHIN players and their wives were waiting to go back to the hotel. Garo and Krikor were not there.

Julie Swift asked, "Are you okay?"

Maritza said, "I'm fine. Where is Garo? Julie said, "He's looking for you."

They got on the bus and went to the hotel. Julie took her to Garo and Doug's room. The wives did not travel with the team. They stayed in a different hotel. In the meantime, Garo left Krikor at the wives hotel in case Maritza and Berj showed up there. Garo then returned to the team hotel and found Maritza. She was in the bed and would stay there the rest of the night. Garo's relatives offered to stay with Maritza but Garo would not leave her to go to the victory party.

The sports reporters were ringing the phone off the hook. There were reports on radio and television that Garo Yepremian's wife had had a miscarriage. Maritza's parent and Garo's parents heard the reports on television and were worried. As soon as Garo and Maritza got settled in the hotel room they called both sets of parents and told them everything was okay.

Garo continued to make sports headlines after each Super Bowl.

The doctors ordered Maritza to stay in bed until her baby was born. Garo was to go to San Diego to practice for five days and then go to Kansas City for the Pro Bowl game on the following Sunday.

Garo said, "I'm not going."

Maritza, "Are you crazy. You should have been in the Pro Bowl last year. You've gotta go this year."

Don Shula said, "You go to San Diego and Kansas City. Krikor can go on the flight and we'll look after Maritza here. She'll be fine."

Garo went to San Diego for the practice and went to Kansas City on the following Sunday to play in the Pro Bowl game. The game was a messy affair. It was extremely cold that day. The ball carriers had trouble hanging onto the ball. O.J. Simpson made a couple of crucial fumbles and was thankful to Garo for getting him off of the "goat's" horns.

On his first field goal attempt, Mel Renfro playing for the NFC conference, slid on the ice as he came across the line and hit Garo on the leg. Garo sustained a hyperextended left knee. He was carried off the field. Back home in Miami Maritza was confined to her bed. She was watching the game on television with her Mom and her friend Violet Vagramian. Violet was the person who told Maritza that there was and Armenian kicker on the Miami DOLPHINS team when she was a student at the University of Miami. When Garo was carried off the field Maritza was terrified. Her Mom and Violet tried to console her.

John Madden was the coach of the AFC team. He asked Garo to kick off on the next play. Garo kicked off and limped back to the bench. In Miami Maritza's Mom and Violet said he must be okay or he wouldn't be playing. Garo's leg was wrapped in ice. On third downs when it seemed that a field goal attempt would be in order they took the ice off and put a hot pad his knee. In the course of the game Garo kicked four field goals in a row. In spite of his effort the AFC was losing 13-12 with :28 seconds to go.

The AFC had the ball and Garo was called on to attempt a 42-yard field goal that would win the game. The kick was good. The final score was 15-13. Garo scored all of the AFC's points. The special teams coach gave Garo a big hug. The loser's got $2500 and the winner's earned $5000.

The coach said, "Thank you my good man. That extra $2500. will put my kid through another year of college."

Garo was voted the most valuable player in the game.

Bob Griese, Nick Bouniconti, Larry Little, Jim Langer and Garo were on the plane flying to Miami when a man who had been drinking too much approached Garo.

The man said, "Great acting job. You pretended to be hurt and then went in and kicked five fields goals."

The man was obnoxious in his alcoholic state.

Jim Langer got up and grabbed the man by the back of the neck and said, "I think you better shut up and sit down. Can't you see that he is going through a lot of pain."

The man sat down and said no more. Garo's knee was badly swollen. The next day Don Shula called

Garo at home and asked about the leg. Garo said it was pretty good.

Shula said, "Did anybody check you last night?

Garo, "There was no one to check me."

Shula, "You'd better go straight to the hospital."

Garo went to Miami's Mercy Hospital and was met there by Dr. Herbert Virgin the team doctor.

X-rays didn't reveal any muscle tears in the knee. Dr. Virgin said he was surprised that nothing was torn. When Dr. Virgin said he would put him in a cast Garo thought he would get a little cast on his knee. When the cast was put on it covered Garo's left leg from hip to toe.

Dr. Virgin said, "We'll check your cast in six or eight weeks and then we'll discuss rehab.

Three days later Garo's leg was itching badly and he was having trouble going to the bathroom because of the troublesome cast from his hip to his toe. He was sitting at his Mom's house when he asked for a chisel and hammer and started cutting the cast. He felt that he had to be able to scratch his knee to relieve that terrible itch. Maritza and his Mom were frightened. Garo massaged his knee and enjoyed a good scratching to get rid of the itch. It felt so good that he went on to cut the cast as far down the leg as he could reach. When Krikor got home he took off the remaining part of the cast. Garo washed his leg and put on elastic ankle and knee supports. He swam in the pool everyday to exercise the knee. Within ten day the leg felt perfect. In two weeks he was in the Orange Bowl with other NFL kickers and got fourth place in the kicking events. Dr. Virgin must have been curious. However, he never asked Garo to come back for further examination. He didn't ask how Garo got out of the cast or what he did with it. The cast is now in Spinelli's, a North Miami Barber Shop. The cast is painted gold. It has a picture attached to it showing Garo being carried off the field in Kansas City along with a picture of his Super Bowl check and some newspaper clipping telling about Garo's selection as the Most Valuable Player in the Pro Bowl Game. Spinelli's is a favorite spot for athletes. Joe Namath got his hair cut at Spinelli's.

Garo's popularity was at a high point. He played Penny Marshall's blind date on the TV sitcom THE ODD COUPLE. He had fun for a week doing that show.

International events also played a role in Garo's off season activities in 1974. In 1960 when Garo and his family left Cyprus to live in London some of his relatives opted to go to Soviet Armenia. They thought they would be able to help their motherland. When they got there they found out that life was not what they thought it would be. Those were the relatives that Garo and Maritza visited in 1971. It took the relatives twelve years to get out of Soviet Armenia. In the spring of 1974 Garo and Krikor made a trip to Cyprus to be Godfathers for the children's baptisms. On the way back from Cyprus in London they picked up an American newspaper. The paper said that Larry Czonka, Jim Kiick and Paul Warfield were leaving the DOLPHINS to go to the newly formed WORLD FOOTBALL LEAGUE. Krikor got excited.

He said, "This is good news for us. Your contract has ended and we have to negotiate a new one."

Czonka, Kiick and Warfield were to get a million dollars each, guaranteed.

He said to Garo, "We'll get on the phone tomorrow. Not that you want to leave the DOLPHINS but they might match any offer you get from the WFL."

The Jacksonville SHARKS were owned by Fran Monaco. When Krikor called him he got excited and asked Krikor and Garo to fly to Daytona, Florida, to meet him. Mr. Monaco picked them up at the airport and drove them to his home in Deland, Florida. He was a very wealthy man and a nice gentleman. Mr. Monaco's wife cooked dinner for them. After dinner while Garo talked to Mrs. Monaco and another gentleman Krikor, Fran Monaco and the head coach went into another room to talk business. After some time they called Garo into the meeting and told him they were offering $300,000 for three years..$100,000 per year plus a $50,000. bonus to sign.

Garo asked, "Is this a guaranteed contract?"

They said, "No. Only the bonus is guaranteed."

While they were a little disappointed that it was not a guaranteed contract Garo and Krikor were happy that they had achieved their goal to get a contract offer in writing from a team in the WORLD FOOTBALL LEAGUE.

It was Thursday afternoon, on the flight back from Daytona they discussed their next move. They wanted to get together with Joe Robbie as soon as possible to tell him about the offer.

When the plane landed they called Joe Robbie's office and was told that he was not there. They then talked to business manager Joe Thomas. They told Joe that they had to talk to Joe Robbie the next day.

Joe said, "You can't do it tomorrow. Tomorrow is Good Friday and you know Joe won't do business on Good Friday."

Krikor then played his best card.

He said, "If he doesn't see us tomorrow we will sign with the WORLD FOOTBALL LEAGUE."

That put a lot of pressure on Joe Robbie. The fans and the press were angry because Czonka, Kiick and Warfield got away from the team. Joe Robbie was forced to meet them the next day.

On Good Friday 1974, Garo, Krikor and Berj went to the he DOLPHINS office to meet with Joe Robbie, Joe Thomas and the team attorney.

Joe Robbie wasn't too happy to hear the Garo had been talking to a team in another league.

He asked, "What is this other league offering you?"

When Krikor told him about the offer Robbie's face turned pale.

He yelled, "I don't believe it. There's no way that anyone would offer you that much money."

In response to Joe's tirade Krikor brought out the written agreement with the Jacksonville SHARKS.

Joe Robbie screamed, "That WORLD FOOTBALL LEAGUE will never last. You'll be without a team before you know it. You want to stay here because the people in Miami like you"

After a long an sometimes loud discussion Joe said, "Are you ready to sign today?"

Garo said, "Yes. That's why I'm here."

Joe, "Here's my best offer. We'll pay you 50-thousand the first year, 60-thousand the second and 70-thousand the third year with a no cut contract. For eight years after this three year contract we will pay you and additional 15-thousand-dollars per year deferred payments.

Garo signed the contract. Garo and Krikor were happy. They felt like they had conquered the world.

In the summer of 1974 a players strike was underway.

After staying in bed for three months after the Super Bowl scare Maritza was able to continue her pregnancy in a normal fashion. Garo was a nervous father-to-be.

On Sunday, July 28th at 7:00 AM Maritza said, "Garo!!" Garo leaped out of bed and stood in front of Maritza.

She said, "My water broke. We've must go to the hospital."

Garo thought of Dick Van Dyke who was in a similar situation during one of his television shows.

Garo said, "Maybe we should wait awhile."

At Maritza urging they drove to the hospital.

Garo went into the labor room with her.

The doctor said, "I think she will deliver in just a little while."

"Doctor, how long will it be?

"Be patient. It'll be over in a few minutes."

The doctor left the room . About every half hour he came back and checked Maritza. The labor pains continued for four hours. Garo feared that she might die.

The doctor said, "We have to take your wife to x-ray. The baby might be too big."

The x-rays were taken. The doctor quickly decided that they would have to do a Caesarean section.

Garo Sarkis Yepremian, Jr. weighed eight pounds,

seven ounces. When Garo saw him he thought he was deformed. His head was shaped like a pear.

Azadouhi said, "Don't worry. He'll be perfect."

Mom was right. Young Garo's head shaped up nicely and Dad was happy as a lark.

Can that much happiness endure the threat of future changes?

Chapter 16 ❧

1974 was a landmark year in the NFL. Due to the prowess of kickers Garo Yepremian and Jan Stenerud the goal posts were moved ten yards back from the goal line and the teams kicked off from the 35-yard line. On field goal attempts that failed the ball was to be returned to the line of scrimmage or the 20-yard line whichever was the most distance from the goal line. Offensive players were not allowed to cross the line of scrimmage until the ball is kicked. Crackback blocks were outlawed. Receivers could only block above the waist. Defensive players were allowed to make only one block on a receiver trying to run a pass pattern. Sudden death was limited to 15-minutes for exhibition and regular season games.

Tampa Bay and Seattle were awarded franchises in 1974 to begin regular play in 1976.

During the season when their husbands were obsessed with football the DOLPHIN wives busied themselves with their children and their charitable projects. Julie Twilly, Judi Griese, Terri Bouniconti and Julie Swift were among Maritza's closest friends.

Most of the players were wound pretty tight. Garo was no exception. The pressures of the game had to be released. Garo couldn't yell at the coaches. They were the generals and Don Shula was the supreme commander. Very few players would dare question their actions.

Garo was tense at home. His occasional outbursts of temper were short lived. His arguments were never carried beyond the present.

Garo was still fearful of air travel. To occupy his mind he played cards in the rear of the plane. Favored people who were allowed to ride on the plane were honored to be invited to play. When Garo won the reporters considered that a good omen.

"How'd you do in the game?" was an often asked question.

In 1974 the DOLPHINS were leading the Oakland RAIDERS in the playoffs after scoring a touchdown with about a minute left in the game. The score was 26 to 20. With 8-seconds left in the game Raider quarterback Kenny Stabler threw a desperation pass that was caught in the end zone. The point after touchdown was good and the RAIDERS won 27-26. It was the last game for Larry Czonka, Jim Kiick and Paul Warfield. They were going to play in the World Football League.

The football seasons came and went. Members of the Broward County, Florida, Police Benevolent Association organized by Bob Morissette formed Garo's army. They sat on the North side of the stadium and chanted Garo, Garo, Garo.

At the start of the 1975 training camp Garo ran five and three quarters of a lap in 12-minute run. He was making an all out attempt to stay in shape. These were the golden years that would never end.

Many banquet stories came out of that period. There was an automobile dealer in Miami who supplied cars for the team. The dealer was invited to fly to Buffalo on the team plane as a guest of the DOLPHINS.

When they arrived in Buffalo the car dealer said to Garo, "I want you to get six or eight players to go to dinner tonight. I'm treating."

Garo, "I think you'll be better off if you only invite three. They eat too much."

Garo called "Dirty" Wally Pesuit. Wally played on the offensive line and weighed about 240 pounds. Wally sported a beard and was a sloppy eater.

Garo also invited Eddie Newman who was his roommate on that trip. Eddie weighed 255 pounds and was the strongest man on the team.

The car dealer, his two friends and the three players went to a fine restaurant. The Maitre d' made a big fuss over the players as he brought out jackets for them to wear. The car dealer was happy.

Dirty Wally ordered two beers, a bottle of wine and a glass of milk.

He said to the waiter, "Bring us some appetizers. Crabs..anything.

When the waiter took their order for the main course Wally asked for lobster. The waiter showed him the live lobster.

Wally shouted, "Is this the biggest lobster you have?

The car dealer said, "Make him the largest lobster you have on hand."

Garo and the auto dealer ordered prime rib.

Eddie Newman ate half of Garo's prime rib and Dirty Wally ate half of the auto dealer's prime rib.

Wally's appetite was legendary. He was known to go to a restaurant and order a rack of lamb for two and then eat it all himself. He was a big man who needed a lot of food to replace the energy he burnt off in the game of football.

He knew how to enjoy food.

The players and other guests ordered a wide variety of desserts and several after dinner drinks.

After the auto dealer paid the check he said to Garo in a low voice, "Thanks for suggesting that I only invite two other players. These guys know how to eat."

Maritza bore a second son on January 27th, 1977. They named him Azad Vartan Yepremian. Azad is the male form of his grandmother's name. It means liberty in English. Vartan is in honor of Maritza's father. Vartan is the name of a famous Armenian warrior and Saint.

In 1977, Joe Robbie bought the Miami GATOS soccer team and renamed it the STRIKERS. Krikor was appointed manager of the STRIKERS. In 1978 Krikor and Joe Robbie couldn't come to terms on a contract. Krikor left Miami and went to New York to be the General Manager of the New York COSMOS. Robbie was livid. He threatened to sue Warner Communications and Atlantic Records the owners of the COSMOS. He didn't follow through on his threat.

Joe Robbie was a man of many moods. In Super

Bowl VII Jake Scott was named the Most Valuable Player in the game. Jake could be moody, too.

The DOLPHIN players were invited to the annual awards banquet. Don Shula and the other players said that attendance was mandatory.

Jake said, "I'm not coming."

There was a large crowd of fans and sports people at the banquet. When number 13, Jake Scott, was introduced he was not there.

Joe Robbie and Don Shula were seated at the head table. Joe had had a few drinks and was in a mean mood.

He said to Shula, "What kind of coach are you? You can't even control your own players. Where's Jake? He didn't even make it to this banquet."

Don Shula and Joe Robbie had a heated argument almost to the point of fisticuffs. Ill feeling developed between them and they talked to each other through secretaries for a long time. Jake Scott was in the doghouse. He was fined. Vince Costello was the DOLPHINS new defensive coordinator. Jake and Vince couldn't agree on anything. Jake publicly disagreed with Vince. They used four letter words and yelled at each other in practice. Don Shula realized that he had a problem. Jake was causing disruption on the whole team. Jake was traded to the Washington REDSKINS. It turned out to be a bad trade for the DOLPHINS. The young player who replaced Jake was unable to perform up to expectations. Garo says Shula was forced to trade Jake Scott because of Joe Robbie's angry fit over the banquet incident.

In 1978, Mike Michelle, a punter/kicker was drafted

out of Stanford University and came to training camp a week early to get some extra practice. Garo read in the paper that the new kicker was doing well.

He said, "There goes another wasted draft choice."

Don Shula didn't appreciate Garo's comments. He didn't like any second guessing about his decisions.

On the first day of training camp Shula said, "Garo, you should do your 40-yard dash now so you can go and kick."

It made no sense to Garo that he should have to do the 40-yard dash. He saw no need for it. He was anxious to go kick with the new draftee. He was determined to run faster than the year before to show that he still had what it takes to be a member of the team. He started the dash and ran a full speed for about 30-yards when he heard a pop and had excruciating pain in his right leg. They helped Garo into the training room.

Trainer Bob Lundy said, "You have a hamstring pull. You'll have to rest it."

Garo rested the leg for two days and it felt fine. He jogged, kicked a field goal and the leg felt good. He kicked a second practice field goal and re-pulled the hamstring muscle. Mike Michelle did most of the kicking in the exhibition season. Mike made the team as a back up kicker and punter. Shula wanted him for insurance in case Garo's leg went bad. Sometimes Mike would make the kickoffs. That took some physical pressure off of Garo. With ice packs and heating pads he managed to complete three out of seven attempts in the early part of the season. His season record was 19 out of 23 attempts.

Early in the season he was three out of seven. Then

he went on to make fifteen in a row. The NFL record was sixteen consecutive kicks.

In the last game of the regular season against the PATRIOTS on Monday Night Football the DOL-PHINS were on their opponents 20-yard line. The team didn't need the points and Shula was going to run the clock out with a ground play. In the sold out Orange Bowl, the fans chanted Garo! Garo! Garo! With six seconds left in the game Shula called time out and told Garo, "Go kick the field goal."

The fans roared their approval. Garo kicked the field goal to tie the NFL record.

As a result of his outstanding record the league's players and coaches voted him into the Pro Bowl game in the Los Angeles Coliseum.

Garo invited Michael Landon, star of Bonanza, to be his guest at the Pro Bowl. He had met Michael in Las Vegas when they played in a Muscular Dystrophy celebrity pro/am tennis tournament. Michael couldn't come. He sent his son Michael, Jr and his father-in-law to the game.

At the DOLPHINS awards banquet before the start of the 1979 season as was customary they showed a highlight film of the previous season's activities. Garo's name was not mentioned in the highlights film.

He whispered to Maritza, "There's something fishy here. I had the best season of my career and tied a league record for successful field goal kicks."

After the film was shown awards were presented to the Most Valuable Player at each position. Garo's name was not mentioned.

He said, "I can't believe this. My own team doesn't

recognize me. I know I won't be with the DOL-
PHINS this season"

That year the DOLPHINS brought in Uwe Von
Shaman as a seventh round draft pick. The team had
big plans for Von Shaman.

Garo worked hard on his physical conditioning.
He did well in the 12-minute run. He actually ran half
a lap extra. That was a first for him.

Garo sensed that something was wrong. The
coaches kept referring to Von Shaman's strong leg.
Garo was not allowed to kick in the exhibition games.
After the fourth exhibition game he decided to talk to
Don Shula.

He said, "Coach, I don't know what's happening. If
you're going to cut me do it now so I can catch on
with another team."

Shula erupted in anger and Garo left the room.

In the final exhibition game of the season Garo
was allowed to kick one extra point after a touchdown.
The next day he was called into Shula's office.

Shula said, "Garo, you've given us nine good years. I
want to thank you for that. You know we have a young
kid with a strong leg. We've decided to go with him."

So there he was. Just before the 1979 season started
he was without a job. The other teams in the league
had selected their kickers and were not likely to give
him a chance.

Garo has always thought that he was penalized
because of the ill feeling Joe Robbie has because
Krikor left him to coach the New York Cosmos soccer
team.

The next few weeks showed that the penalty was
for long and sinister yardage.

When the news of Garo's dismissal broke the radio, television, press and fans in the Miami area were in an uproar. Garo had a terrific season the year before and now he was no longer with their team.

Don Shula was unable to give a satisfactory reason for Garo's dismissal. It was unreasonable to think that the most recent Pro Bowl kicker could be cut without having had an opportunity to perform in the pre-season games. To make matters worse he was cut just before the season started after other teams had made their choice of kickers.

As the days went by and no team called for his services. Garo came to the conclusion that he was being punished because of Krikor's fight with Joe Robbie. He felt that he was being blackballed from football.

To add to the fan's dissatisfaction Uwe Von Shaman missed an extra point and had a field goal blocked in the first game of the season.

The Seattle SEAHAWKS came to Miami for the first home game of the season. Joey Carr, Garo's friend in the advertising business, insisted that he go to the game. Garo, Maritza and Joey drove to the Orange Bowl in a limousine. Garo was in disguise wearing a fisherman's hat and dark glasses.

Maritza says, "It was a crazy time."

As the game went on the DOLPHINS' new kicker wasn't doing well. The fans began chanting Garo! Garo! Garo!

Unbeknown to Garo Joey had hired a man to parade around in the stands with a sign that said "GARO"

Several other Garo signs appeared.

In the third quarter a reporter discovered Garo

sitting in the stands. The television camera focused on him while the announcers reported his presence.

The next evening on Monday Night Football Howard Cosell was giving the highlights of that weekend's games. When Howard gave the results of the Miami-Seattle game he spoke in the measured cadence of his most pontifical voice.

Howard said, "Who should be sitting in the stands but the Tiemaker-Tiebreaker Garo Yepremian. Why is a kicker of Garo's caliber sitting in the stands? He should be kicking for an NFL team."

Howard Cosell brought new life to Garo's career. The telephone rang.

PART 3 ❧

PART 3

Chapter 17 ?̀

H oward Cosell's Monday Night Football sug-
gestion that Garo should be kicking in the
NFL caused results.

The next day the New Orleans SAINTS called.

The SAINTS personnel director said, "We need you
to come to New Orleans. Get on a flight tomorrow."

Garo asked, "Where do I stay?"

He said, "Stay at the hotel across from the airport.
We can't tell anyone you are coming until we make
some moves with our personnel."

In the days immediately following his cut from the
DOLPHINS Garo hired an agent. When he got the
call from New Orleans Garo told the agent not to call
any other teams. Two hours later the agent called back.
He sounded worried.

He said, "Garo, I don't know about New Orleans.
They told me they were having you in for a tryout."

Garo flared in anger, "Why did you call them. I
told you not to call any other team."

All of a sudden Garo was worried. He wasn't sure of the job. He decide to call New Orleans.

He said, "I'm not coming for a tryout. I have proven myself for the past 12 years in the NFL."

The personnel director said, "No, we want you as our kicker."

Garo replied, "I found out from my agent that I'm coming for a tryout on Tuesday."

The man replied, "Look, I didn't know he was your agent. A lot of people call us and ask who we are bringing in for a kicker. We told them we are bringing in a few kickers. When they ask about you we said you would be one of them. I assure you that you will be the kicker. There will be no tryout."

Garo went to New Orleans on Thursday and reported to the SAINTS camp. The SAINTS announced that he would be their kicker.

When he arrived at camp he was told that the doctor would give him a physical. Garo was worried. If he didn't pass he wouldn't make the team.

The doctor said, "Bend backwards. Bend forward. Bend to the side."

Each time Garo did a bend the doctor would ask if it hurt.

He asked, "Did you ever have any operations?

Garo said, "No."

The doctor was amazed. Garo had played for 12 years and had no serious injuries.

In the back of his mind Garo was worried. He feared that his groin or hamstring muscle might give out.

The following Sunday the SAINTS played the 49ERS at Candlestick Park in San Francisco. Garo was called to attempt a field goal in the third quarter. It was a 24 yard attempt. This was an important opportunity for Garo. He had tied the NFL record for consecutive field goals with 16 in the previous season. This one would give him a new NFL record. As he ran in to take his position for the kick he saw that the ball was going to be placed down on the pitching mound area. The rest of the field was very soft and Garo was wearing long cleats on his right foot. He knew that those cleats were wrong for his kick from the dirt of the pitching mound.

Garo said to the holder, "Call time out."

The holder was nervous. He was the third string quarterback. He was shocked. He had never heard of a kicker calling for time out. Usually the defensive team calls time out to give the kicker time to get nervous. Garo turned to the referee and gave the time out sign. He didn't want to jeopardize his kicking string and the team needed the three points.

Garo ran to the sidelines. Dick Nolan, the head coach was as confused as the others over the un-expected time out. Garo quickly changed his right shoe for a rubber cleated shoe. He then ran in and kicked the field goal. He broke the record for con-secutive field goals in the NFL.

Garo went on to kick three more to end his string at 20. His 21st attempt was slightly blocked in a game against the Washington REDSKINS.

On the Thursday before the Washington game he injured his hamstring muscle. The SAINTS had another kicker, Rich Czaro. on the injured reserve list. When he saw Garo wince he was happy. He figured that he would be reactivated.

Garo went into the training room and wrapped his leg in ice.

Whitey Campbell, the special teams coach came by and asked, "How are you feeling?"

Garo, "I have a pulled muscle in the kicking leg. I can still kick. It has happened to me before. I will kick through it."

Whitey said to Garo, "Big man, you are a proven pro. You don't have to kick during the week."

Whitey had confidence in Garo. Czaro was not reactivated.

Garo's painful routine began in the morning when he would get up and go to camp and get into an icy whirlpool bath. There was lots of excruciating pain. After fifteen minutes in the icy bath he would get out and plunge into the hot whirlpool. The alternate cold and hot baths improved the circulation and promoted healing. After the whirlpool treatment he would go to the team meeting and following practice to be with the team's players. He did not do any kicking during practice. After practice Garo went home and Maritza would have ice packs ready for his leg.

The SAINTS allowed their players to spend Saturday night at home. That was good for Garo because he was required to practice his kicking on Saturday. On Saturday evening's his leg throbbed with pain.

Friends came in from Miami to see the game. Garo could hardly walk to the car.

He said, "Don't worry. Under the pressure of the game I will be OK."

Inside he was very concerned. He wasn't worried whether or not he would make a field goal. He was worried that he might collapse on the field. Shooting pains ran down his leg with every movement. Garo believes that as a professional player you are not pampered. Each player must look out for himself. He toughed it out. "Shook it off" as the coaches say about the players when they overcome horrendous injuries. Garo was the SAINTS kicker for the remainder of that year.

Garo made a lot of friends on the New Orleans SAINTS. In October during the World Series he won some money in the clubhouse baseball pool. Garo gave a hundred dollars to the trainer.

Garo said, "Get some Popeye's Chicken."

The trainer said, "One-hundred dollars worth?"

Garo, "Yes. If you have some money left get some beer."

That was on Thursday the regular weigh-in day for the players. The offensive linemen were very important to Garo. They protected him on his field goal attempts.

He said to the linemen, "You better run into the clubhouse. I've bought chicken for the players."

The team had a party with the chicken. On the following Sunday they won their game.

On Tuesday after the winning game the five team captains met with coach Dick Nolan. They told Nolan that they wanted to repeat the chicken party. The captains suggested that the fine money be used to buy the chicken. That's how "chicken day" became a team institution for the SAINTS.

Garo had three homes during this period. He had a house in Miami that he couldn't sell and a new house that he had bought while a member of the DOL-PHINS team. He rented a house in New Orleans.

After the 1979 season his leg began to feel stronger and most of the pain was gone. Garo's and his friend

Joey Carr from the advertising agency went to California to meet with Michael Landon. Michael promised Garo a part in one of his LITTLE HOUSE ON THE PRAIRIE television shows. The night before the appointment to see Michael Landon they went to the La Scala restaurant. While they were waiting in the bar area someone came from behind Garo and covered his face with their hands. Then Garo was lifted off his feet by this giant and was carried around in the restaurant. They passed Jacyln Smith's table. She was one of the stars in CHARLIES ANGELS. Garo didn't know who was carrying him. The people in the restaurant were laughing. When the man put Garo down to his amazement he saw that the funmaker was Lyle Alzado who had played with the Denver BRONCOS and later with the Oakland RAIDERS.

Lyle said, "What are you doing tomorrow night?"

Garo, "We don't have anything planned."

Lyle, "I want you and your buddy here to come to dinner with me. I want you to meet my agent Greg Campbell. We'll be having dinner with Linda Ronstadt and the Hudson Brothers."

Garo was excited. He wasn't sure what was going to happen. The dinner was to held at an Italian restaurant. Garo thought that possibly Linda Ronstadt and the Hudson Brothers might be performing there. When Garo and Joey arrived at the restaurant they were taken to a private room with a long table that could seat about twenty people. More people came and the table filled up.

Joey turned to Garo and said, "Where the hell is Linda Ronstadt."

Garo replied, "I think that is Linda across the table."

Joey wanted to have his picture taken with Linda. She refused. She was dating Jerry Brown, Governor of California at the time, and was wary of any photo opportunities.

During the meal Lyle Alzado suggested that Garo hire Greg Campbell to negotiate his next contract with the SAINTS. Garo decided to accept Greg's offer.

He said, "I would like to have more money and a no-cut contract."

In the negotiations with the SAINTS Greg did get more money for Garo.

The SAINTS business manager said, "We can't give him a no-cut contract but we can guarantee that he won't be cut."

Greg said, "Give Garo a 25-thousand-dollar loan at no interest to be paid back in a year. But, if you cut him during training camp he won't have to pay the loan."

Garo signed the contract and felt good about the deal.

At the 1980 season training camp Russell Erxclaban the number one draft choice the year before had a one-million dollar no-cut contract as a kicker and punter. He had been hurt the year before that was why Garo was signed by the SAINTS. Erxclaban reported that he was fit to play. Garo outkicked him in practice but because of the SAINTS commitment to Erxclaban Garo was let go. He did not have to pay the 25-thousand-dollar loan.

Quarterback Archie Manning, Safety Tommy Meyers and Middle linebacker Joe Federspiel called Garo in and said they were sorry he was cut. Stay in shape. We have a feeling that they will be calling you back. If they don't they are crazy.

Garo went back to Miami.

Maritza asked, "Are you going to call any teams?"

Garo, "No. Most probably New Orleans will call me back. That kid can't do any kicking."

The next morning a representative of the Tampa Bay BUCCANEERS called. Garo was invited to come to Tampa Bay and demonstrate his kicking ability.

When Garo got in the cab at the airport in Tampa Bay the cabdriver said, "You are Garo Yepremian. You are the third kicker to come through this airport this week; Jan Stenerud, Jim Turner and you."

Garo thought, "Why am I here?

When Garo arrived at the BUCCANEERS camp he was met by Phil Kruger special teams coach and personnel manager.

He asked Garo, "How far can you kick?"

Garo, "I can make anything inside the 50-yard line. I kick my field goals in 1.2 seconds."

Phil Kruger smirked. The average speed of a kicker was 1.3 or 1.4 seconds.

They went onto the field and Garo performed just as he said he would.

Phil said, "If it were up to me I'd sign you right away. I have to wait for Coach John McKay. He's playing golf."

Half an hour later McKay returned and Garo was signed. He would play on the following Sunday.

Garo could have gone back to the New Orleans SAINTS if he had waited another week. Russell Erxclaban missed a 21-yard field goal and the SAINTS lost to their arch rival the Atlanta FALCONS.

After the game Russell walked into the coach's office and said, "I can't kick anymore field goals. I want to concentrate on punting."

The SAINTS had to find another kicker. They picked up Benny Ricardo from the Detroit LIONS.

Garo played with the BUCCANEERS for the remainder of the 1980 season. There were a few things that bothered him about the atmosphere on the Tampa Bay team. Coach McKay insisted that the players report to the team office on the days when they were leaving for an away game. He would then put the offensive players on one bus and the defensive unit on another bus for the short trip to the airport. This was quite different than the "we are one" team spirit on the DOLPHINS and to a great extent the same spirit on the New Orleans SAINTS team.

The BUCCANEERS were the underdog against the New York GIANTS. The BUCCANEERS won the game. Garo thought that coach McKay would be happy and give them a morale boosting talk in the clubhouse after the victory. After one of the offensive linemen led the team in the post game prayer John McKay talked about how the players had to learn to stay behind the yellow line on the side of the field. During games he was in a constant state of agitation while yelling at the players for going over the line.

On a plane trip from Los Angeles to Tampa Bay the players were given their usual six pack of beer. A lot of players drank the beer to combat the dehydration of the game. Garo drank a can and a half and gave the other cans away. While the plane was in flight Garo needed to go to the bathroom. The other players told him he should stay away from the rear of the plane because Coach McKay was in a foul mood after the loss of the game. He would yell at any player passing his seat. The players were not allowed to use the bathroom in the front of the plane because the owners wives were seated up there.

Garo said, "I don't care what he says. I'm thirty-seven-years-old and I have to go to the bathroom."

Garo walked to the rear of the plane as he went by McKay seat he saw that McKay was fast asleep.

Garo noticed that none of the other players went to the bathroom. Some of the players had consumed large quantities of beer.

Garo asked, "How do you guys drink all that beer and not go to the bathroom?"

The reply, "The beer cans serve the purpose after we empty the beer."

Garo thought, "Wow, you guys are recycling your beer."

Fierce football players are putty in the hands of a strong-willed coach.

Garo spent the off-season in Miami where he continued to be a fan favorite. The legendary DOL-PHINS are revered by the people in Miami.

Garo reported to training camp and kicked his way through the exhibition season.

On Sunday September 20th, 1981 the BUCCA-NEERS went to Chicago to play the BEARS. Chicago beat Tampa Bay 28-17. Garo kicked a 32-yard field goal in the fourth quarter. That was his last kick in professional football.

On his way to practice on Wednesday, September 23rd he heard a sports reporter say the he had been cut from the BUCCANEERS. Garo was angry and hurt because he had to hear on the radio that he had been released.

When Garo arrived at the field he went into McKay's office where he got the official bad news. Coach John McKay said his kickoffs were too low and too short.

Garo was angry.

He told reporters, "The team is like an automobile that's having transmission trouble. The mechanics are changing a tire on the car. Changing the tire represents action but it won't fix the transmission."

The decision had been made. Garo was out of football. He expected other teams to call him.

The call didn't come. Garo rationalized that there would be other things for him to do.

The pain of rejection was compounded because Friday, the 25th of September was Maritza's birthday. Garo knew that his problems would cast a gloom over Maritza's birthday happiness.

The always optimistic Maritza said, "Let's go to Tarpon Springs and celebrate. A new chapter in our lives is just beginning."

Garo thought there would be offers coming in from everywhere. He would do commercials, give motivational speeches, maybe even be an analyst for football games on the network. He was shocked. No one wanted to hear from him. No one sought him out to be a spokesperson. He went into a shell of embarrassment and self-pity. At thirty-seven years of age Garo was washed up in football. What could he do?

Chapter 18 ❧

Garo sat there in the kitchen of his house in Miami. He knew he had to snap out of his mental funk and do something. In his reverie he thought about the carefree days in Larnaca, Cyprus and the sheer enjoyment when he kicked his soccer ball against the church wall. Memories of the wall helped him work through his early fears with the LIONS. When hostile crowds and teams tried to make him nervous by calling timeout before his kick attempts his thoughts of the wall made him smile and kept him relaxed. Big dreams and super success were his companions on those mental flights of fancy. He had exceeded those dreams and risen to unimagined heights of popularity and personal intensity as he out played the college star challengers who threatened to topple his world.

Garo's fears were similar to those of a miser who hoards money and denies his family the simple pleasures of life. The miser has a secret fear of having to go back to the orphanage where he spent his childhood. With Garo it was fear rooted in the turmoil of the past that haunts most Armenians. After reaching star status in the NFL Garo achieved some comfort and family stability as a citizen of the United States. He had done it in the face of tremendously improbable circumstances.

His recovery from celebrity status would be a slow and painful process.

Garo's younger brother Berj worked for Chapman Auto Security.

Berj said, "Garo, you love the automobile business. You should come and see Mr. Chapman and go to work for his company."

Garo agreed to call Bob Chapman.

When he arrived at Chapman Auto Security he said, "Mr. Chapman I would like to come and work for you. I'm out of football, you know."

"Garo, you are a celebrity. You're a star. Will you work five days every week? We have a position open in Broward County that will require you to visit six auto dealers each day."

"Look Mr. Chapman, if I weren't prepared to work I wouldn't be here. I played football for fifteen years. It was fun. Many other players weren't as lucky as I. Now it's time for me to move on to something else."

Garo sold auto security systems for two years. While he felt betrayed by the NFL teams he enjoyed the friendliness of the auto dealers. It was easy for Garo to set appointments with the owners or general managers of the automobile dealerships. He kept up a good front smiling as much as necessary.

Maritza was Garo's unfailing supporter. She helped him on his worst days.

During his football years she'd say, "I know it wasn't your fault. You'll have a better game next week."

When Garo went on road trips she would hide notes in his baggage.

"Dear Garo, I love you very much. You are going to have a good game. I am praying for you."

Garo worked for Chapman Auto Security for two years.

In 1983 Garo was asked to narrate a twenty-five minute Community Guide, Incorporated, presentation. It took him two days to finish the project. It was interesting work. The company had plans for Garo. They asked him to come and see their operation. Garo liked what he saw. He left Chapman Auto Security and joined the advertising company. He had to go to Pompano Beach for a week and study from 7 A.M. to 6 P.M. It was an hour-and-a-half drive from Garo's home in Miami to Pompano Beach. After a week of study Garo started making presentations to professional people and businessmen. Garo had the magic touch. He made six presentations a day and averaged four sales. He was the company's number one salesman by far. He drove a big Mercedes Benz and had a car phone.

After a year of sales success in the advertising business Garo discovered that the company secretary was making fourteen to sixteen appointments for him every day. They sent other salespeople to the extra appointments. The sales people would make excuses about why Garo couldn't be there. They said he was tied up in traffic or had car trouble. Garo didn't like that. He decided to get out of the business. He told his sales manager that he was leaving because it was too far to drive to Pompano Beach. The advertising company asked him to start his own operation in Miami. Garo opened the Miami office and lasted for six months. He was tired of the business and got out as soon as he could.

In the meantime Berj started his own company after leaving Chapman Auto Security. He sold auto alarms, stereos and operated a glass tinting service. Tinted glass was popular due to the hot Florida sun. Garo visited Berj's factory. He noticed that there was not much business and that the company wasn't doing very well. Garo remembered his years as a fabric cutter in London. He used his experience to create a pattern for a reversible automobile floor mat. That was a unique idea. Two ladies were hired to do production work. One was from Nicaragua and the other from Cuba. The mats were custom made with several colors of piping to suit the individual customer's needs.

Garo worked long hours at the factory. He was happiest when he didn't have time to think about his glory years in the NFL. Maritza, young Garo and Azad worried about Garo. They thought he was working too hard. Within six months the business was growing. Garo found another location in Coral Gables, Florida, where he opened a factory and a retail store in the same location.

One day a young man about eighteen years old came to the factory begging for work. His name was Alvaro Funes. He was from El Salvador and desperately needed a job. Although Alvaro looked a little frail Garo liked him. Alvaro got the job. Alvaro worked hard and was honest. Garo gave him a little more responsibility each month. Eventually Alvaro became manager of the factory while Garo concentrated his efforts on sales at the retail store.

Earlier, when Krikor went to New York to be the General Manager of the New York COSMOS soccer team Garo was honorary National Chairman of the Hemophilia Foundation. He followed actor Richard Burton as National Chairman. In the course of his chairmanship he attended a banquet in New York. Garo stayed at the Park Plaza hotel. At the banquet he met Patricia Mulay who was a worker on one of the hemophilia foundation committees. Garo got her telephone number and gave it to Krikor. He knew that Krikor was alone in New York and the Yepremian brothers always looked out for each other. Krikor called Patricia and that started a love affair that ended in marriage.

Patricia had two chocolate shops in New York where she sold chocolate from Taucher's, a well-known Swiss chocolate company. She had a store in the Park Plaza and another one at the Waldorf Astoria. After Krikor and Patricia were married they started their own chocolate company. They hired a chef and opened the company in a warehouse on Long Island.

Eventually Krikor and Patricia moved to Oxford, Pennsylvania. Their two sons, Nicholas and Alexander, attend school in the Oxford area.

In 1986, Bob and Judi Griese accompanied Garo and Maritza to Super Bowl XX between the Denver BRONCOS and the New York GIANTS at the Rose Bowl in Pasadena, California. They were there to finish a feature piece for SPORTS ILLUSTRATED.

Judi Griese was very happy at the game and showed no signs of illness. Less than a year later she died after being ravaged by breast cancer.

Late in 1988 Maritza underwent a routine mammogram test. The mammogram didn't show anything, however, the doctor decided to do an ultra sound study. A mind numbing discovery of Maritza's breast cancer hit Garo with a sledge hammer blow. His first reaction was anger.

"Why Maritza? Why me."

Anger turned to frustration. There were moments of hope and long periods of despair. Garo was between insurance policies and did not have insurance to cover the cost of an operation.

The doctor said, "Wait. You can have the operation when you get the money."

Garo didn't want to wait. He remembered Judi Griese at SUPER BOWL XX. Don Shula's wife Dorothy was also being treated for breast cancer and was not doing well.

Maritza entered Baptist Hospital in Miami in January, 1989. She had a lumpectomy and the doctors reported that they had gotten all of the cancer. It had not spread to other parts of her body.

Maritza and Dorothy Shula went to the hospital for follow up treatments. Six months later Dorothy died as a result of the dreaded breast cancer.

Maritza's Mom lived with Garo in Miami. She had been a woman with so much energy and enthusiasm. She developed Alzheimer's disease and didn't recognize anyone. Maritza took care of her for three years. Maritza became exhausted both emotionally and physically. They hired a full time nurse who worked from 8 A.M. to 5 P.M. for $500. per week.

This was a time of stress and depression for Garo's family. The Florida heat took its toll on Maritza. The local environment was bad for their sons. Crime was on the increase and daily tension was a common thing.

Maritza suggested that they leave Florida. Garo, Maritza and the boys had visited Krikor in Oxford, Pennsylvania, the year before.

Young Garo and Azad said, "Let's move to Oxford."

Garo thought, "There's no way I can live in a little village like Oxford."

August 2nd, 1990 was Krikor's fiftieth birthday. Garo and his family visited Krikor in Oxford.

While they were driving through the town to go to Krikor's house Garo said in jest, "Maritza, would you like to move to this little town?"

Maritza looked at him and smiled.

She said, "I'd love it. That would change my whole life."

Garo said, "Let's ask the kids."

"Boys how would you like to live in this little town?"

The boys yelled in unison, "Yes! Yes! Yes!"

At dinner that night at Krikor's house Garo said, "We're thinking of moving to this area. Is it too close to you?"

Krikor was thrilled.

"No, no, it will be wonderful to have you nearby."

The next morning Krikor called a real estate office in Oxford. The real estate man came with pictures and maps. He showed them several homes. At first they couldn't find anything they liked. They didn't want to have to remodel a house. The next day Krikor spoke to his attorney about Garo's desire to relocate in Oxford.

The attorney said, "I know just the house for your brother. No one has looked at it."

Garo and Maritza inspected the house and fell in love with it. They met with the real estate man and negotiated a price that pleased them as buyers and the seller was happy, too. They agreed to send the down payment when they got back to Miami.

Another worry reared its head for Garo. He didn't want to tell Azadouhi and Sarkis that he was leaving Miami. He worried about his Mom seeing the for sale sign in his yard. He told Azadouhi that it would take a long time to sell the house. In his own mind Garo knew that he had to sell the house within three months. He couldn't afford to have two mortgages at the same time. Two weeks later the real estate company set up to have an open house at Garo's place. The real estate lady showed up an hour late and there wasn't much buyer activity.

Garo said to the real estate salesperson, "Leave the signs with me and I'll have open house every Sunday."

Garo lowered the price of the house by $45,000 and sold it within two weeks.

Garo told his Mom that the house was sold and that she should look on the bright side.

He said, "You and Dad can come visit us in Oxford. If you like it we'll help you move there to be near us."

Mom was still concerned about Garo and his

family leaving Miami but his comments about joining them in Oxford help ease her fears.

Krikor and Patricia lived in a two-hundred year old farm house. Early in December the house caught on fire and was severely damaged.

Two moving vans left Miami with Garo's household furnishings. When they arrived in Oxford a heavy snowfall was underway. Only one van was able to unload at Garo's house. The other van couldn't get in because of the heavy snow.

Garo and his family moved into the Nottingham Inn near Oxford. The snow storm ended and the moving van was able to unload the rest of the furniture. Garo, Maritza and the boys moved into their new house. Krikor and his family moved in with them. It took four months to get Krikor's home back into livable condition.

Garo was the family cook. He gained weight from inactivity. He began to take walks in the town each evening. On one gray afternoon he went to a park. There was no one around at the time.

Garo thought, "This feels like the twilight zone. Maybe I'm dead and just here for a return visit. Am I crazy for moving here?"

Later when Garo expressed his feelings Maritza said, "Wait until next year. I know you'll say it is great here."

Maritza goes to the Hospital of the University of Pennsylvania every three months for follow up tests due to her breast cancer. She has passed all of the tests with a clean bill of health and is becoming happier each day. The good medical reports give Garo hope for the future.

He says, "Thank God, the doctors got it all. I thank God every day that we didn't wait for the operation."

He began to reach out and attempt to make friends in the media.

He also decided to learn to play golf. He attacked the game with gusto. It didn't take him long to lower his scores from 118-120 to the respectable 80's. He went on to play in the Vince Lombardi Tournament in Milwaukee, the Bryant Gumble charity event in Florida and the Mike Schmidt and Richie Ashburn tournaments in the Philadelphia area. Garo is a fan favorite and spends a lot of time signing autographs. Garo feels like he is back in the land of the living.

Chapter 19 ࣷ

In March 1991 Garo traveled to Lancaster and met with the Program Manager of WGAL-TV. He was an NFL fan and was familiar with Garo's exploits on the field. They talked about the famous "pass" that Garo tried to make in Super Bowl VII. Garo's personality struck a responsive chord. Garo's style would please an audience. There was nothing available at the time. They promised to call him if an opportunity arose whereby WGAL could use Garo's talent.

About a year later there was an opening for a co-host on a WGAL daily live talk/variety show. Garo was asked to come and audition for the role.

The audition was a set up. Jim Berman, the station's research director posed as a man who was trying to have his father pardoned from prison. The father had committed a mercy killing of his wife a few years earlier. Jim Berman is a superb actor. He was convincing in his role. Garo handled the interview with compassion and skill. He asked questions that brought out the love of the interviewee for his father even though he was terribly aggrieved at the death of his mother. The interview was so poignant that the producer and director who set up the make believe interview felt pangs of guilt. Garo obviously thought this was a real life situation. His interview touched a wide range of compassionate emotions. He was a finalist for the job at WGAL.

Garo's father and mother visited him in Oxford over the Christmas holidays in 1991. During that time Sarkis suffered a heart attack and was hospitalized. When he was discharged from the hospital he and Azadouhi stayed at Garo's house. In January 1992 Sarkis suffered another heart attack and died in Garo's arms. It was a sad time for this close knit family. Sarkis who, as a four-year-old boy, fled with his mother to escape the wrath of the Turkish soldiers and worked as a shoeblack to prevent starvation died in Oxford, Pennsylvania, in the midst of his loved ones. Garo and his family cried in private and gained support from each other.

The next day Garo hid his grief. He arrived for his final job interview at WGAL. He was offered the position and immediately accepted employment as the co-host of a daily LIVE talk/variety show.

The exposure on WGAL opened several doors of opportunity for Garo. WGAL held an outing at a sports bar in Lancaster for clients who would be participating in the sponsorship of the Olympics. Garo was the featured speaker at the event. Dan Boyle was among the business men he met. Dan is in the furniture business. Dan founded the BED AND FURNITURE WAREHOUSE company in the early eighties. His store is a no-frills set up and overhead costs are kept low. Dan is able to pass on the savings to his customers. In the beginning, Dan worked hard, took some financial risks and built his business into a successful venture. When Garo met Dan he had two stores in Lancaster County, Pa.

Dan Boyle is thankful for his success and is anxious to give something back to the community. He has supported several charities and wants to do more. Dan learned that Garo gave motivational speeches that explain how he overcame improbable odds to play in the NFL. Dan saw an opportunity to work with young people in a positive way. He sponsors Garo's talks in local high schools. Dan and Garo go to the schools and talk to the principals and teachers. Most of the time the school principal remembers Garo from his glory days in the NFL. When the school passes out flyers to the students about the coming speech by Garo Yepremian it is amazing how many young people are aware of Garo as an ex-NFL star. Football card collecting is a big hobby nowadays.

On the day of the speech Garo goes to the school cafeteria and mingles with the students and signs autographs. After lunch the formal assembly program usually draws a large number of students. Garo tells about the handicaps he had to overcome to play in the NFL. His diminutive size compared to most of the giants in the NFL was one of his handicaps. His lack of football experience in high school and college did not stop him. Garo stresses the importance of education in today's highly competitive world. In summary, his speech says that with the right attitude, desire and willingness to work, young people of today can reach any reasonable goal that they set for themselves. He overcame his handicaps and reached the top without resorting to drugs or alcohol for false courage.

All ex-athletes think that if given an opportunity they can do it again. The roar of the crowd is never forgotten. It is the elixir of life for an athlete. Garo is no exception. He sees today's NFL kickers miss field goals shorter than 30-yards.

"I can make ten out of ten from 30 yards."

Nelson Sears said, "Garo, talk is cheap. It can't be that easy."

"Ok. I'll prove it. Let's go to the high school field." After a doing stretching exercises and a few warmup kicks Garo performed like a kicking machine. Garo, Jr. was the holder and Azad shagged the ball on the other side of the goal posts. Kick after kick cleared the cross bar.

"Garo. You're amazing. We can't let your kicking skills go to waste."

We'll arrange for you to do a half time show. Ten companies will have an opportunity to sponsor one of your kicks. If you make the kick the company will donate $100,000 to charity. On the 10th kick you will move back to attempt a 40-yard field goal. If you make the 40-yarder each of the sponsors will pay double."

A week later I awakened at 4:20 A.M. from a dream filled sleep. I began to fantasize about my dream for Garo. I knew that Garo slept with his portable phone within reach. I dialed his number.

A sleepy voice answered, "Hello, who's this?"

"Garo, I've had the most fantastic dream about

you. I'm going to write about it. I'll bring it to you
this evening. Will you be home?"

"OK. It sounds intriguing. I'll be here."

Over the preceding year-and-a-half Garo became
accustomed to my calls at any hour of the day or
night.

This is what I wrote.

In the dream, a news release was sent to the local
media. A prophet has no honor in his own country.
The announcement is met with sincere apathy. The
local sports writers and broadcasters are more interested in the off-season antics of the high-salaried
darlings of the day.

Garo talked to Dan Boyle about it. Dan got excited
and offered to sponsor a kick. The MBNA bank
wanted in on it. A soft drink company, a candy maker,
Keystone Associated Auto Dealers and the Uni-Marts
company agreed to be sponsors.

Garo's friend Joey Carr, owner of the Joseph L. Carr
advertising agency in Miami Beach whipped up
enthusiasm among the former "Garo For Quarterback"
club members. They bought shares in a sponsorship
for one kick. The money was designated to go to the
Muscular Dystrophy Foundation. They agreed to make
a donation no matter what happened on the tenth
kick. Joey did a good job. He was a faithful friend and
supporter. When Garo was with the New Orleans
SAINTS and broke the record for successive field goals
Joey Carr was the one who called sportscaster Dick
Shaap in New York and arranged for Garo to be
interviewed on the TODAY SHOW.

The dream continued. The kicking exhibition was
sold out in a hurry after Greg Gumble mentioned it on

ESPN. Advertising agencies are ever alert for good opportunities to improve their client's brand awareness in the marketplace. Network sports producers smelled a good story and the buildup began. Garo appeared on CNN on LARRY KING LIVE and was quoted in newspapers all over the country.

Late in 1993 Rupert Murdoch's FOX TELEVISION NETWORK bid 1.58-billion-dollars and was awarded the contract to carry the NFC Conference games beginning in 1994.

The executives of FOX TELEVISION said, "We paid the NFL big dollars because we saw an opportunity to bring our network into parity with the big three, NBC, CBS and ABC."

FOX bought the rights to the kicking exhibition. They would show it on the network just before its telecast of the first regular season NFC game. This is a story with no down side. It is a quadruple-win situation.The charities will be winners. The sponsors will get terrific exposure for their money and the fans will see an event that is truly unique in the annals of sport. Garo will hear the roar of the crowd. He will put an exclamation point on his football career-a career that seemed incomplete following his days of depression after his unexpected cut from the Tampa Bay BUCCANEERS.

When news of Garo's unique kicking exhibition spread throughout the football fraternity the telephone calls began to come in. Several of the legendary DOLPHINS offered to hold the football for Garo. Dr. Doug Swift, former DOLPHINS Super Bowl linebacker, called from his home in Philadelphia. Bill Bergey, the former Philadelphia EAGLE, offered to help. Like kinfolk in a Louis Lamour western novel Garo's former teammates are willing to ride in and help their friend. They doubted that fifty-year-old Garo could make the ten field goals but they couldn't resist the opportunity to be in the action once again.

In the dream, Garo went into training.His routine was not as strenuous as Don Shula's twelve-minute run but it did have its moments. Garo walked at a fast pace, jogged a little, watched his diet and lost about twenty-five pounds. Watching Garo work to get back into shape was pleasing to Maritza. She worried about his health in general. Maritza could tell that the tension was beginning to build and that Garo needed her support more than ever.

She taped a note to the steering wheel of Garo's car.

Garo unfolded the note and read, "Dear Garo, I know you are working hard. I know your dream will come true. You will be successful in your kicking exhibition. I love you now and will love you forever no matter what happens."

Garo felt the excitement. This is the chance of a lifetime to win back his honor and his self esteem. He quietly went to his recreation room at home and saw his Super Bowl trophies and old NFL uniforms. Many great athletes finish their careers with a team or teams that are not the one they played on in their glory days. In his heart Garo would always be one of the legendary DOLPHINS. Three Super Bowls and the record setting 17 wins and 0 losses in the 1972 season were fond memories.

Garo yelled for Maritza to come to the rec room.

"Maritza, which uniform do you think I should wear when I do the kicking exhibition?"

"Garo, there's no doubt in my mind. Wear the DOLPHINS uniform. That's the one you were wearing when I saw your first game in Miami."

That clinched the decision. In spirit and in his former team uniform he would be a DOLPHIN once again.

Spring blended into summer. Garo celebrated his fiftieth-first birthday on June 2nd, 1995. He intensified his training regimen and spent most of his evening hours kicking the football into the practice net in back of his house. When Garo, Jr., and Azad were home they practiced at the high school field. Garo enjoyed kicking toward real goal posts.

Garo took one weekend off in June to participate in a charity golf tournament for the Urban League of Lancaster County, Pa. The news of his forthcoming exhibition was beginning to spread. The players and fans at the golf tournament asked questions about his kicking ability.

Garo said, "Come to Veterans Stadium in Philadelphia and I'll show you that I'm serious and intend to earn a lot of money for those charities."

Game day finally arrived. Garo, Maritza, Garo, Jr. Azad and Mom Azadouhi left early Sunday morning to go to the stadium. Krikor, his wife Patricia and their sons, Nicholas and Alexander rode in a separate car.

Garo was assigned a space in the Philadelphia locker room. Maritza and the other members of his family went to their seats a few rows up from the fifty-yard line. In the locker room Garo put tape on his right ankle. The tape would give his ankle needed support when he planted his right foot on the artificial turf of

Veterans Stadium. He sat quietly on the bench in front of the locker. He moved to the sideline when there was about 10 minutes left in the second quarter. He did his warmup kicks into a practice net on the EAGLES side of the field.

The game is being televised in Philadelphia and on a regional network.

During the two-minute warning timeout the sideline announcer positioned himself with Garo in the background. After the first play in the final two minutes the officials took time out for a measurement. The TV director cut to a shot of the sideline announcer who told his viewers that Garo Yepremian the legendary DOLPHINS kicker was going to attempt the impossible at half-time. At the age of fifty-one he was going to kick ten field goals in a row, nine from 30-yards and a final kick from 40-yards.

Following the rule that there are no dumb questions by a working reporter he stuck a microphone in Garo's face and asked, "Garo, what causes you think you can do it?

"I didn't come here to miss, thank you."

The half ended and the EAGLES trotted off the field. On his way to the locker room some players came over and "slapped five" with Garo.

The Public Address announcer said, "Ladies and Gentlemen. The specially appointed official at the left goalpost is none other than the last man who played 60 minutes in an NFL game, the EAGLES own Chuck Bednarik."

There was a loud round of applause as the ever-popular Bednarik from Bethlehem, Pa. ran onto the field.

"On the right hand goalpost former EAGLES linebacker Bill Bergey."

Both of the former EAGLES were wearing green EAGLES tee shirts.

The PA announcer continued, "Retrieving the footballs behind the goalposts this afternoon are Garo's brother Berj Yepremian, Garo, Jr. and Garo's second son, Azad."

As their names were announced they ran onto the field clad in DOLPHINS tee shirts.

"And now, to hold the ball for today's 30-yard attempts former EAGLES quarterback Ron Jaworski."

Another loud burst of applause ensued.

"Now sports fans, here to do his best for charity and to prove that age is a state of mind it gives me great pleasure to introduce the kicker of the decade of the seventies, a veteran of three Super Bowls and a legendary Miami DOLPHIN forever, the great Garo Yepremian."

Garo ran on the field carrying his helmet and waving to the crowd. He took his position two steps back at a forty-five degree angle from the ball. Garo's adrenaline was pumping full force.

The PA man said, "The first kick worth one-hundred-thousand dollars is sponsored by the Bed and Furniture Warehouse in Lancaster Pennsylvania."

Garo raised his hand and brought it down to his side. He approached the ball and hit it cleanly with his left instep. The ball rose and cleared the crossbar near dead center. The officials, Bednarik and Bergey raised their hands overhead to signal that the kick was good. With the first kick successfully completed Garo relaxed and felt confident. His next three attempts appeared to be easy as he continued his routine. After each kick the retrievers ran to the sideline and presented the football to a representative of the sponsoring company. On the fifth kick something happened. It could have been a bit more pressure applied to the ball by Ron Jaworski's fingertip. It may have been a slight misalignment of Garo's foot against the ball. The moment he hit it Garo sensed that it was not a perfect kick. His kicks normally start out to the left and then hook in to go between the goalposts. This time the football went a little too far to the left. The crowd gasped and then applauded as the football hit the left goalpost and ricocheted toward the center and crossed the bar.

Garo turned his back to the goalposts, took off his helmet and breathed deeply to regain his composure. He thought, "I can't let these people down. I've got too much at stake here to mess up now."

He thought about other crucial points in his career when the going was tough. He breathed a prayer asking for help in this his crucial moment in life after football. As usual when he said his prayers he felt relaxed and was able to do his best. The next four kicks were easy as he "got in the zone" as athletes often say when they are at the top of their game.

When the ninth kick cleared the cross bar Ron Jaworski jumped up and shook hands with Garo. Garo put his arm around Ron and thanked him for a job well done.

He said, "Ron, you haven't lost it. You are still a great professional and a credit to the game."

The Public Address announcer's voice boomed throughout the stadium, "Ladies and gentlemen, Garo

Yepremian will now move back for the tenth kick of the afternoon. This will be a 40-yard attempt. If he makes this kick each of the sponsoring companies has agreed to double its donation to the Muscular Dystrophy Association. This is a large bonus for the MDA if Garo is successful."

The PA announcer continued, "And now to be the holder for this important kick it is a pleasure to introduce the man who made it possible for Garo to come to the United States and kick off in the first football game he ever saw. Here is Garo's older brother Krikor Yepremian."

Krikor dashed onto the field in his DOLPHIN tee shirt waving to the crowd as he carried the football to the 30-yard line. He knelt down to place the ball in position and thought of the early days when Garo kicked an American football for the first time when they practiced in an attempt to get Garo enrolled in Butler University. Krikor thought of the tryout for the Atlanta FALCONS and the success that same week when they went to Detroit and signed with the LIONS. This was a "lump in the throat" moment for brother Krikor.

In the stand near the fifty-yard line Maritza was frantically waving her orange scarf. It was the same one she used to signal to Garo in the old days at the Orange Bowl in Florida. Garo saw the fluttering orange scarf and tapped his helmet two times to signal that he knew that Maritza was watching and praying for him.

Garo held his left hand high to signify that he was ready. The crowd grew quiet. He lowered his hand and approached the football. The moment his foot hit the ball Garo knew that it felt good. He watched the flight of the football and heard the roar of the crowd. In his mind the ball was powered by the crowd as it spun end over end and left the stadium to become the spirit of football. The ball travelled near the speed of light. It circled over Larnaca, Cyprus and flew by the church wall that meant so much to Garo in his quest to become a football star. The ethereal ball continued on it way and rose high in the firmament. It traced a sign in the heavens to serve as a beacon of hope for all people. If you look though the telescope of imagination into the sky on a clear night you can see in the dim stars of the Milky Way that there is a replica of Garo's wall stretching across the heavens. It is there to show that it is possible to overcome impossible odds to achieve an honest goal in life.

The football passed through Canton, Ohio to spin its way over the Football Hall of Fame as it made the return trip to Veterans Stadium in the summer of 1995.

Resuming its earthly form the football dropped over the crossbar dead center between the goalposts. Bednarik and Bergey raised their hands to signal success. Garo heard the tremendous roar of the crowd. Interviews and television appearances and the congratulations of his family and friends were heaped upon him. He knew that his National Football League career was finished forever.He was ready for the challenges of life that lay ahead.

EPILOGUE

I arrived at Garo's home in Oxford at the end of a bitter cold February day. In the cozy warmth of the family room his wife and sons gather around while Garo reads what has been written about my dream. With tears in his eyes his subconscious and innermost feelings were impossible to hide.

Garo speaks, "God has given me mental and physical powers to overcome many obstacles. The true purpose of this dream is to show that I must continue to motivate others to have hope, inspiration and ambition to reach their goals.

My speeches at hundreds of school assemblies show that young people have a deep-seated hunger for words of encouragement. The business people who support my work know that the future of the world is in the hands of our precious children."

His voice trembled with emotion, "Maritza, I know how to make this dream come true in a symbolic way. Each time a message comes from someone who says that I have helped them I will know, in my heart, 'I keeked a touchdown.' "

THE END